What Time Is It? You Mean Now?

Advice for Life from the Zennest Master of Them All

YOGI BERRA

with Dave Kaplan

SIMON & SCHUSTER

New York London Toronto Sydney Singapore

SIMON & SCHUSTER
Rockefeller Center
1230 Avenue of the Americas
New York, NY 10020

First Simon & Schuster trade paperback edition 2003

Illustrations © Alan Dingman

Book design by Ellen R. Sasahara

For information regarding special discounts for bulk purchases,
please contact Simon & Schuster Special Sales at 1-800-456-6798 or
business@simonandschuster.com

Manufactured in the United States of America

1   3   5   7   9   10   8   6   4   2

The Library of Congress has cataloged the hardcover edition as follows:
Berra, Yogi, 1925–
What time is it? you mean now?: advice for life from the
Zennest master of them all/Yogi Berra with Dave Kaplan.
p. cm.
1. Berra, Yogi, 1925–   2. Baseball players—United States—
Biography.   3. Baseball coaches—United States—Biography.
4. Conduct of life.   I. Kaplan, Dave, 1956–   II. Title.

GV865.B4 A3 2002
796.357'092—dc21
[B]   2002030213

ISBN 0-7432-3768-4
0-7432-4453-2 (Pbk)

Contents

What Time Is It?
You Mean Now?

A

"I **Ain't** in a Slump. I'm Just Not Hitting."

I think your life depends on your attitude. How you face things says a lot about you and about how people treat you, a lot about what you can do and can't do, a lot about your happiness or unhappiness. You are what you think; maybe that's why some people need attitude adjustments.

Nobody can be all smiley all the time, but having a good, positive attitude isn't something to shrug off. It starts right when you wake up—for me that's six o'clock—and you can almost tell if it's going to be a good day or a miserable one by how you feel in your head. There are lots of things in life you can't control, but how you respond to those things is the one thing you *can* control.

I always believed in myself, believed in my abilities. Everybody in baseball—everybody in life—goes through periods where you can't seem to do anything right, where it's easy to get down on yourself or get discouraged. If I wasn't hitting, I figured that I just wasn't hitting, not that I couldn't hit. I didn't learn how to hit in a day, and I wasn't going to forget how to hit in a day, or even a week. That's how I kept myself positive, by not getting all negative.

I try to accomplish something each day. Do something good. I work out almost every morning, and that makes me feel like I started the day right. Honestly, everybody has a bad day, but usually you can think of something that you did that was OK, so the day wasn't a total loss. If I wasn't hitting, I could still help us win by how I worked with a pitcher from behind the plate. Today, if things are going wrong around the house, maybe it's a good day to work on the lawn or to paint the shutters. As long as you keep doing stuff, your luck might turn.

Being part of the Yankees for so long, I can tell you that attitudes get passed down. Our teams from the late 1940s through the early 1960s had great camaraderie and a winning attitude. Even today you don't see guys on the Yankees moping or whining or blaming other people when things go rotten. In the 2001 World Series, Derek Jeter was having it tough because his shoulder was injured pretty bad, but he never used it as a crutch, or even mentioned it, or expressed his frustration. I think he knew that worrying about it or blaming his injury would hurt his own positive attitude, and the team's.

The best way to deal with any bad situation is to believe in yourself and have confidence that things will get better. After all, if you don't believe in you, why should anyone else? Baseball is a game of confidence, and of overcoming failures and fears. That's what life's about, too. I found that out early on as a teenager, when Branch Rickey told me that I'd never be a major-league player after a tryout in my hometown of St. Louis. I was pretty disappointed, that's for sure, but I kept a positive attitude because I thought I was good enough to make it. That rejection only made me more determined, and a year later, the Yankees signed me and things worked out OK.

Two years after that, I was in a pretty tough place, in the Navy as part of a six-man crew on a LCSS (Landing Craft Support Small) for the Normandy invasion. Our job was to shoot at the German gun emplacements to protect the troops wading ashore behind us. I understood the danger, but there really wasn't time to be scared. We worked like the devil to keep the boat moving so it wouldn't be a target. We got shot at, but we were never hit. I remember saying to myself that I was only nineteen, I'm too young to die. That's how you had to think.

The saying about turning a negative into a positive . . . well, I think it's true. I always look on the brighter side. My family still jokes about when I drove them up to Cooperstown for the first time. I said that we were lost, but at least we were making good time. Same thing when I was managing the Mets and we were in last place: I said it ain't over till it's over, and we made it to the World Series. I guess that was my attitude and it still is.

"**Baseball's** Different Today, But It Isn't."

Baseball's a great game. It's kind of a symbol of America. It doesn't matter where you're from or how big you are, anyone can play it. If you commit yourself and love it enough, you can find a life in baseball because it's a big industry. Baseball is actually like life because it's pretty unpredictable: One day you can have a heartbreaking loss, the next day you bounce back, as long as you work at it and don't panic. You need dedication and discipline, and sometimes you need more luck than skill, because you can get a bad break and weird things can happen. When you think you've got it figured out, in baseball sometimes you find you don't know nothing.

I think baseball is still the national pastime, the best game there is. It's passed down from generation to generation, brings people together. And you meet a lot of great people through baseball—at least, I sure did. To me, the game's almost perfect—dirt, grass, fresh air, it just feels right. How did they know 90 feet was the right distance between bases? Or that the pitcher's mound to home plate was right, too?

As a catcher I loved being in every play. I liked studying everything, trying to outthink the hitter, working in harmony with the pitcher. Catching two no-hitters by Allie Reynolds in one season, and Don Larsen's perfect game in the World Series, those meant as much to me as anything I could've done on my own. It was being part of the teamwork that made the results so rewarding.

Concentration's the key in baseball. I didn't think too much at the plate because I was concentrating. And I never saw anyone with more intense concentration or inner drive than Ted Williams. He was great to play against because I loved the challenge of competition, loved going against the best. You get focused on your job, but you can always have fun, too. I'd talk to a lot of the hitters, Ted included, just to chat and be friendly, ask them about their family, what they were doing after the game, whatever. As long as they didn't mind, I'd keep it up. I don't think it bothered their concentration, at least they never said it did. Those guys I played against, they're still my friends, because baseball really is a big brotherhood.

The game gets in your blood as a kid and stays there. When you say strike, I think of a pitch that's chest or belt-high; I don't think about union lawyers or owners' lawyers or that stuff, and I wish it could be the same for kids today. Baseball is about history, tradition, and strategy. To me, the beauty of baseball is that it goes back to your childhood. It consumed me as a kid, I couldn't get enough of it. Still can't. I always try to watch a couple of games a night. As a fan you can forget your worries, because any kind of baseball is a good way to relax.

It's a game made for stories—there's nothing more enjoyable than telling old baseball stories. Of course sometimes you can't separate what's real or not real, there are so many myths, but that's the fun of it, too. I have trouble believing some of the stuff I hear about me. You'd think I was funnier than Bob Hope with everything I supposedly said or did. I don't know how I say some of the things I do—they just come out. I guess the truth is I'm out for fun, but I'm kind of serious about it.

Some of the guys from my playing days still love the game, and some don't. Baseball's still the same game, even if it's gotten a little different. The worst things? Artificial turf and designated hitters—I could do without those. Managers who overmanage, too—they just make too many pitching changes nowadays. There are too many playoff games. And the World Series shouldn't always be at night—they're losing young fans. Some of my lasting memories of childhood are listening to the World Series, but if kids can't watch it today, how are they going to remember them?

I don't know if players are any better today, but they sure are bigger and stronger, some of them even look like bodybuilders. I just hope they love and respect the game and the fans like we did, because that's what matters. It's no secret that the ballparks are smaller and some of the old hitting records are being shot to hell, but that's OK—statistics and records are good, but they're always going to be broken. The hitting's good these days because the pitching isn't. There are just so many teams, and so many pitchers are rushed to the big club well before they're ready. In our time there were fewer teams and the competition was greater—we had guys like Eddie Lopat and Vic Raschi, who couldn't even make the majors until they were in their late twenties.

There probably should be less teams, that might solve some problems. But the players won't go for it, because they'll lose jobs. Plus they don't trust the owners, and the owners think the players make too much money—and they make a lot, that's for sure. But don't cry for any owner—they aren't going to the poorhouse, either. Why would they be in the game in the first place?

Am I worried about baseball? Why, what can I do about it? The thing is, it's a great game and has always weathered major problems. The Black Sox scandal almost killed it, but didn't. Babe Ruth (and the souped-up ball didn't hurt) helped save the game in the 1920s. The game survived World War II, and it's survived lockouts, free agency, teams moving, you name it. It has to be a great game to keep surviving and going.

It's a different life these days. Baseball's different, too, and it isn't. In the 1940s and 1950s, we had fun. They called it the Golden Age, and it was incredibly competitive: only eight teams in the league and there was always someone ready to take your job. I never dreamed we'd accomplish so much, but hunger accomplishes a lot of things. Funny, there's so many different things to do these days—there's so much technology, so many different choices. Back then, we didn't have as many distractions or choices. We took to baseball. There wasn't so much else. Things were simpler. The game is simple, but it's never easy. Maybe that's why people still love it.

"If You Can't Imitate Him, Don't **Copy** Him."

I'm not sure what charisma is, but you can tell it when you see it. Some people are just different; they've got an aura, although you really can't see an aura. People with charisma are usually liked, respected, and admired; you respond to them in a good way. Most of the time, I guess.

It's hard to describe. When I was a coach with the Yankees in the 1970s, Thurman Munson used to always tell me I had charisma. I didn't know what the heck he was talking about. Maybe people liked me, but I don't know about any aura. Truth is, I think Thurm had some good charisma. He was gruff and tough and had a blocky body like me, but there was something different about him that everybody respected and that made him a leader. Probably his charisma.

It's a rare quality that you don't see too much. If you don't have it, you probably never will. It's something most leaders have or want. Without it they're sunk, because it's a power that gets people's attention.

Charisma is a star quality, but it's something that's somehow endearing to everybody. It shows them as real people. Michael Jordan is the world's best basketball player, but when he tried baseball he failed pretty good. That made him seem more human without hurting his charisma one bit.

I think Princess Diana and President Kennedy had good charisma, too. They were real popular, that's no secret; they came from money, they had good looks, and they both died tragically. But they had appeal around the world because they had a common touch. They connected to the less fortunate. They didn't act bigger than they were.

Golf wouldn't be where it is today without Arnold Palmer. Arnie may have more charisma than any sports figure anywhere; he made people want to watch golf in the 1960s because people really cared about him. He was no robot, just a regular guy giving everything he had on every shot, just like any hacker. Plus he has an honest personality and always mingled with the gallery. He always made them feel like he was one of them.

Golf wouldn't be where it is without Tiger Woods, either. He's one guy I always wanted to meet, and I was real glad when I did at a big *Sports Illustrated* century thing a couple of years back. But his charisma is different. There's a magic about him, but you don't see Tiger smile much after a good shot. When you're that good, I guess you don't have to. Still he has a remarkable presence; he's one guy people die to see.

I think charisma gives off a good, positive emotion. People are naturally drawn to those who have it; look at Babe Ruth—he was like Santa Claus. Look at some boxers—Muhammad Ali and Sugar Ray Robinson and Jack Dempsey. I bet each of them could've drawn a crowd on the North Pole, they had such great style and appeal about them.

I was fortunate to play with two of the greatest players in history, Joe DiMaggio and Mickey Mantle. And both had bushels of charisma. DiMag was the shy, silent hero—people thought "hello" was one of his longer conversations. But the way he acted and dressed, real elegant with those tailored suits, made people look up to him. He had an image of class, and everything he did showed his charisma. I heard a writer say he began idolizing him just by the way he ate his spaghetti.

But his charisma rubbed off on all of us, too. He was one heck of a leader. Like I say he never said much, but he led by example. He played hurt, expected you to do the same. He was real proud of being a Yankee and expected you to be, too. All he'd have to say before a game was, "Let's go," and you'd feel a boost. On and off the field, he had grace and charisma—we always looked up to him.

Mickey had different charisma, but he had a lot of it. He was more one of the guys than DiMag. He had his fun, and he had good looks, too. And he could hit the ball to the moon. Everybody loved Mickey; people would flock to every ballpark to see him play. Funny, when he first came up, he was real shy, too. You couldn't get a word out of him with a can opener, but that changed. Carm and I thought one of the great things about Billy Crystal's movie *61** was how it showed Mickey's confidence and charm. You could see how beloved and generous he was as a teammate. Sure he had his faults, but nobody had star power like him.

It's not a fair thing, this charisma stuff. One guy has it, another doesn't. Muhammad Ali sure had it; not many of his opponents had it. You can't manufacture it, and you can't fake it. But sometimes it's overrated, especially in management. It doesn't take someone full of charisma to make his business a success, and our Yankee teams were proof.

Our general manager, George Weiss, was a pretty grumpy, conservative, no-frills guy who was obsessed with every detail, even the brand of toilet paper used in the locker room. He built and oversaw the Yankee farm system. He was a perfectionist and a workaholic. He was also a hard-nosed negotiator, and all he cared about was making money and winning championships. Charisma? Forget it. But the guy was successful as hell. When I was managing the team in 1964, the team was bought by CBS and then run by Mike Burke. He was tall and dapper, a World War II hero, and had lots of personality. But charisma can only take you so far, because the Yankees went downhill real fast.

"Are You **Dead** Yet?"

Death is one of those things in life nobody likes to think about. When you get older, you think about it more, but it's not good to dwell on. When people ask me if I'll be playing in a golf tournament next year, I say, "If I'm alive." I don't mean anything by it, I'm just trying to be honest, because you never know.

Death is a terrible thing—you can't ignore the sorrow of it. I've lost a lot of good friends, many of them gone too young. Nothing really prepares you for it, either. When my parents died, relatively young, it hit me hard. I still carry a remembrance of them every day.

Those of us who went through World War II saw enough life and death to put everything in perspective, especially things like sports. My mom was so worried about me in the service, she lit a candle and prayed every day. When I returned, I didn't want her to know I was supposed to get a Purple Heart, because that would've worried her only more. She didn't need to know what it was like.

They say baseball is like life, but it sure isn't life and death. Unless you count the crazies who think it is, like the lady fan who shot Eddie Waitkus, who played for the Phillies way back. I've heard of some fans who get ulcers over baseball—I can't understand that. Most players don't. People get too emotional about the game. Maybe that's why they call them die-hards; I don't know.

People everywhere die all the time, many of them too soon. Sometimes the threat of dying shows someone's true courage. I never met Lou Gehrig, but his farewell speech still gives me chills—he called himself the luckiest man on the face of the earth, and he was dying. When the Yankees had a special day for me in 1959, Carm and I wanted to do something to honor his memory, so we sent the proceeds of the day to Columbia University, where Gehrig went to college.

It was awful to see Catfish Hunter, one heck of a great guy, die from the same disease. Cat also had diabetes, but you never heard him complain, not once—I can't imagine how much pain he felt, or Mickey Mantle, either. I was proud of Mickey because he did something great in his last days, warning kids about drugs and drinking.

Maybe it's true that death can bring out the best in people. One of the best baseball movies I've ever seen is *Bang the Drum Slowly,* which is sort of about death. Robert De Niro played a catcher—Johnny Bench actually trained him—who used to get ragged on by his teammates. Then the De Niro character got a serious disease, and the players changed how they treated him. They showed a real human side. The player eventually died, but it wasn't a tearjerker because his teammates learned to appreciate him and life even more.

A number of years ago, Joe Garagiola went on his crusade against spit tobacco because he got tired of seeing players get cancer and die from it. Showing pictures of these guys who'd lost part of their faces brought it home to the young guys. They learned to respect life more, too. Joe taught them a powerful message.

Everybody has to die some time, but the big thing is to take care of yourself—cherish life, get the most out of it. Losing loved ones is always hard because it's the end—it's final. I did tell Carm, though, that she ought to put on my tombstone, "It's over."

I'm not sure what it is about death that always fascinates people. A couple of years ago, reporters heard Whitey Ford had some cancerous lesions removed, and they kept trying to call him, but nobody heard from him, and all I heard for days was, "How's Whitey? How's Whitey?" Finally I called him up and said, "You dead yet?" Whitey appreciated it because he knew what I meant. He was fine, he just didn't feel like talking to strangers about it.

Truth is, I don't really like talking about it, either. It's just that it comes up a lot, and I try not to let it bother me—I try to think of positives. When Carm's mother died recently, it was real sad because she was a terrific lady. Fran Ferlauto, our secretary at the museum, asked me her name because she wanted to send Carm a card, but I didn't know. I always called her Mom.

I'm lucky that Carm is a very upbeat, positive person and doesn't dwell on this stuff either. One time, though, she did ask me where I should be buried. Our families are from St. Louis, where I grew up; my career was in New York; we live in New Jersey. I told Carm, "I don't know, just surprise me."

"It Gets Late **Early** Out There."

Around World Series time, the sun in left field at Yankee Stadium would get awful tough. It wasn't so bad during the season, but in October it would just hang there in your eyes when you were trying to follow a fly ball. And what was true for the sun field in the Bronx is also true for everybody when it comes to their bodies and their health: You can get old pretty young if you don't take care of yourself.

Everybody needs exercise, I don't care who you are. Exercise is the best medicine, unless you're really sick and need something else. It's the best way not to feel old and fat, plus it's great for your mental health. Staying in shape, working out on the treadmill, and playing golf a lot are the best things that happened to me after I retired from baseball.

I feel OK, and people keep telling me I look good for

my age, and that makes me feel OK, too. I like being active, and I pace myself because it feels crummy to feel worn down. Getting up at six every morning and doing different activities keeps me going, and so far, so good.

A lot of older people—people like me in their seventies—are living longer and healthier lives. Older people travel more, walk more, run more—heck, they even do marathons and hike mountains, like some people I know. They're doing things that seemed impossible only a few years ago. Being sixty-five used to seem like old age, but more and more guys I know feel pretty good when they get there, and they're willing to get physical therapy or medical help in order to keep exercising.

Look at today's athletes—not that they're senior citizens or anything, but these guys, and even the gals, care more about exercise and fitness than ever. That's something we never did. We only got in shape during spring training, but these guys work out year-round and you can see a difference in their longevity when they last longer. Nolan Ryan and Roger Clemens, they have those great workout ethics, which keep them as strong as ever when most fastball pitchers used to be slowing down. And Barry Bonds going from thirty-something home runs to seventy-three in two years tells you a lot about his health. He got real serious about it, using a nutritionist and a new workout regimen. You got to be serious about it or you can't expect good results.

A lot of people and athletes overdo it, though, so you

got to be careful. Some of these guys are always getting some pulled muscle because they have more new muscle. It's not just about getting bigger, but getting bigger in ways you can use—stretching, flexibility, all that stuff. Every team today has fitness coaches—something we never had—and the players do more exercises, are bigger and stronger and mostly in better shape than ever before.

But while more older people are exercising, one big problem we have exercise-wise is kids. They need exercise, but they don't; they play video games or get stuck in front of the TV and the computer. Most kids in their teens aren't real active, and the truth is, you see a lot of overweight kids these days. This affects their bone development and probably raises their chance for heart problems. When we were their age we just played outside all the time. Kids may need a push to exercise, and if it's safe and enjoyable, it will help make them feel better, think better, and do better.

There's a good connection between exercise and an active mind. Look at Stan Musial, one of the best ever. He took over for my idol, Joe Medwick, on the Cardinals in the 1940s, and he's always been one heck of a guy. He was part of the reason I met Carmen, because she was a waitress in Biggie's restaurant, which Stan once owned with Biggie Garagnani.

My point is that Stan loved to play ball; he was a ballplayer's ballplayer, always in great shape, always a great attitude. I remember grumbling to him in the twelfth inning of the 1955 All-Star Game how I was getting tired catching all those innings. And Bill Summers, the umpire, said, "How about me? It's just as tough back here." And Stan said, "Yeah, I'm tired, too," and then smacked the next pitch over the wall and we all went home.

Stan went on to play until he was forty-three and a grandfather. Boy, he could hit, too. Everybody liked him, and President Kennedy really admired him. Kennedy told him once, "A couple of years ago they told me I was too young to be president and you were too old to play baseball, but we fooled them." When Stan retired, Lyndon Johnson appointed him director of the President's Council on Physical Fitness, and he set a real good example for kids, talking about the importance of exercise and all those other important things kids need to know.

Stan is in his eighties now, and he hasn't lost any enthusiasm, and I think his exercising all the time helped him beat cancer ten years ago. Like I said, enjoying old age is half mental, half physical, and remaining active helps you remain active.

"When You Come to a **Fork** in the Road,
Take It!"

Everybody's got fear. Everybody's afraid something bad is going to happen sometime. That's life. But what's important is that you don't let it stop you from doing things, taking risks. Every decision is a risk, every choice leaves a choice behind. You can't let yourself get paralyzed by the fear of what might go wrong.

Fear is a big part of everything we do. There's fear of failure, fear of flying, fear of getting hurt, fear of doctors, and so on. When I got my knee replaced a few years ago, you could say I had a little fear. What if something bad happened? What if the doctor screwed up? Thing is, I knew I wanted to walk without pain and play golf pretty bad, so I went through with it, a little fearful but I went ahead anyway. Fortunately everything worked out pretty good, and the harder I worked in rehab, the better I felt. Now my knee is great; they say I won't have to replace it for another fifteen or twenty years, but that's OK because I figure they'll have to replace me first while the knee keeps on going.

There's a lot of people with phobias, that's just the way it is. Phil Rizzuto was—and still is—one of the great worriers; he's afraid of everything that moves. Mice, insects, snakes—anything that crawls he's afraid of, which is why he was a great target for pranks. Guys would put worms in his glove and he would jump ten feet. Phil also had a real fear of birds, and once Johnny Lindell put a live bird inside a drawer where Phil put his valuables when he dressed for the game. He put his hand in the drawer and felt the bird move and tore out of the room like crazy. I don't think he ever used the drawer again.

My biggest fear is probably death; I know I'm going to die, but I don't especially want to be there when it happens. If I have another fear, maybe it's more a dislike, it's public speaking. I don't mind answering questions in front of a large group, but giving speeches is something else. It just makes me uneasy; it's just one of the best things I hate.

I guess we all have some kinds of fears. The trick is to overcome them. It really comes down to confidence and concentration. Baseball's a real good example: A lot of young kids have a fear of getting hit by a ball. Why? Because when it hits them, it hurts. The main thing is to teach them how to hit properly, and how to get out of the way of an inside pitch. Using a tennis ball to practice is a good help, because you can gradually build up the confidence and lessen the fear.

It's funny, but a lot of kids think they can really get hurt playing baseball. They don't worry about getting in a fight or falling off a skateboard—but they're still afraid of a little ball. Truth is, the chance of getting hurt by a baseball is really, really small. But the fear exists . . . even for big-leaguers.

Reggie Jackson never lacked confidence, except when it came to Nolan Ryan, who he said was "the only guy who put fear in me. Not because he can get me out, but because he can kill me." I think Randy Johnson scares some guys in the same way, too. He's so big, throws so hard, I think there are many guys just plain afraid to hit against him. That's not good for your confidence.

As a hitter, I always thought I had the advantage: I had the bat in my hand. I hit against some guys who threw real hard—Bob Feller and Herb Score were real fast—but I honestly never feared anyone. Maybe the one guy who made me a bit nervous was Sandy Koufax when he first came up. We'd see him in spring training and he had no idea where the ball was going. That wasn't good for your confidence, either.

President Roosevelt said there was nothing to fear but fear itself, and that makes sense to me. Whenever someone goes to a hospital or has an operation, I always try to cheer them up. My granddaughter Lindsay is a fearless kid, real athletic, but she had to get a hernia operation and was pretty worried. When I asked her what the heck was she worried about, she looked at me like I was crazy and re-minded me how nervous I was before my knee operation.

So maybe the truth is you can't get rid of people's fears, but you can help them go on despite them.

Not everybody's always helpful. Looking back, I feel kind of bad when I think about Jackie Jensen, who was a good player and briefly a teammate on the Yankees, and was terrified of flying. We'd be asleep on a plane, and Billy Martin would grab an oxygen mask and yell, "Jackie, we're going down!" and it really shook him up. Jackie never overcame his fear of flying and it cut short his career.

You have to appreciate people who struggle to overcome their fears. Jimmy Piersall was a real good player for the Red Sox, but he had a nervous breakdown because he had all sorts of paranoid fears—they even made a movie about him called *Fear Strikes Out*. The good thing was that Jimmy eventually got better, got his confidence back, and played a great centerfield. He always stayed a bit flaky, though. How many guys used to take bug spray to the outfield?

"You've Got to Be Careful If You Don't Know Where You're Going Because You Might Not **Get** There."

If you don't set goals, you'll never reach them. Or like they say in golf, if you aim for nothing, you'll hit it every time. Take any player in the major leagues: I'd say just about every one of them had a dream—a goal—to be a big-leaguer when they were kids. It wasn't an easy goal, but it was a reachable one, and that's important.

Becoming an overnight billionaire or the fastest runner in the world aren't such reachable goals. You can dream, but that's about it. Goals are different than dreams. Goals have a time limit and an action plan; dreams don't. You can dream forever and never get anywhere, but goals you can reach. Goals are for movers, not mopers.

As a catcher, my goal was to get my pitcher to reach his goal. If a pitcher was in trouble, you'd go out to talk to him. Well, he already knows he's in trouble, so he doesn't need you to tell him that. Mostly all you do is try and calm him down, but different pitchers need different treatment. With Whitey Ford and Vic Raschi, I'd try to get them mad. I'd yell at Raschi, "Come on, Onionhead, throw the ball," and he'd swear at me but would bear down. With a Bob Turley, you've got to baby him. Tell him he's got great stuff, he can do it, and if he gets this out, we're going to an early movie.

Mostly my goal was to get the pitcher to concentrate by making him relax. When Joe Page, who was a real good reliever for us, was in a jam once, I went out and asked him if he had any kids. He looked at me crazy and said, "No, I don't. Why?" I told him that he had to have kids, it's the best thing for a family. He started to laugh, and it must have got him to relax, because he retired the side.

Everybody has goals, or they should, because that's how you improve or feel better or get to where you want to go: losing weight; going to a good college; swimming fifty laps a day. Just don't let anyone else set your goals—you do it yourself. Only you know what you want, and only you know what's realistic.

I was fortunate to get to be the only thing I ever wanted to be—a ballplayer. Baseball was my goal as long as I can remember, but it didn't come easy. I quit school after eighth grade to go to work, but I was still determined in my mind to play ball. The first job I got was in a coal yard, which got me real dirty all the time. I'd vanish at three o'clock, find a ballgame to play in. Soon I became a helper on a Pepsi-Cola truck, but lost that job, too, because that was a summertime business and I ran away to play ball too much. After that I got a job in a shoe factory, making $17 a week, the most money I'd ever seen, and it went straight to the household. But that also interfered with my ballplaying, so I quit again.

You could say I was pretty intent on my goal. When I was sixteen and playing American Legion ball, I learned to play all nine positions. When I tried out for the St. Louis Cardinals that year, I was told my best chance was as a catcher. Then they told me I had no future in baseball, and that kind of left me a bit heartbroken. But I felt I was still good enough and young enough, and a year later the Yankees signed me to a minor-league contract.

Honestly, I think the longer you take to decide what you want to do, the more you're just wasting time. Just know where you're going or else you might not get there.

Most kids are pretty sharp and pretty goal-oriented. They know what they want to be and God bless 'em. When some tell me they want to be baseball players, I don't discourage them; I just tell them they better want it bad and work at it real good. Challenge themselves and don't be afraid to fail. And I tell them if they don't make the majors, they can be productive and successful in many other ways. Mostly, they should set proper goals; their goals should be their goals, not someone else's. Parents have goals for their kids—mine wanted me doing anything but baseball—but it should conform to the kids' potential and their wants.

I think goals define your ambitions. But once you reach

them, don't stop. Celebrate if you do what you set out to do—I bought my parents a car with my first World Series check—but then set new goals and keep going. Raise the bar, and keep pushing yourself. Once I got to the majors, I really didn't set personal or specific goals in terms of statistics or anything like that; winning three MVPs was great, but my real goal was to stay in shape, play hard, and do whatever it took to help the Yankees win. Personal goals or milestones weren't big for any of us, and that's why we were such a good team. Our only goal, really, was to get into the World Series every year—and win. Being the best and getting that check were the big things. I always remember my backup, Charlie Silvera, encouraging me: "Keep going, Yogi. I need that World Series money. I want to build a new wing on the house this winter."

When you reach a goal, I guess there's a tendency to ease up. Casey Stengel tried to motivate us after we won the championship in 1949 by saying the next year would be harder because it's very difficult to repeat. Then when we won in 1950, he said the hardest thing is winning three in a row. After we won our fifth straight, I guess he realized we needed no motivation—we had the same motivation every year. Our goal in spring training was to win the championship every year. The bottom line is that goals need to be serious wants, and you've got to be willing to put in the work it takes to make them happen.

"Ninety Percent of This Game is **Half**-Mental."

One of the great things about baseball is that it teaches you humility. Every time you think you're pretty hot stuff, you're usually reminded you're not. Every time you come to the plate, 70 percent of the time you'll fail. Every time you think you're going to win, you can easily lose. Every time you're awarded an honor, there's others out there more deserving.

I think humility means never forgetting where you came from and who you are. It's been said that I have pretty good humility, though I never did say, "It's not the heat, it's the humility," which is another one of those sayings people say I said. Truth is, someone once told me that "humble" is a word that means "being close to the ground." So being short and squatting all those years behind the plate, maybe that's how I got a little humble.

I've always considered myself just a kid from The Hill in St. Louis. That was the neighborhood where I grew up, a place of tight-knit Italian families who scrapped and worked every day to put food on the table. It's like a lot of neighborhoods where, no matter what you become later in life, it's still the place that stays inside you. It's where you get your pride and determination, just like Sammy Sosa and Pedro Martinez got growing up in the Dominican Republic. They're both great baseball players, both multimillionaires, and they still have that modesty and ability to care about others that's great to see.

One of the best people I ever got to know was Catfish Hunter, who was a great example of never forgetting who he was. Cat signed one of the first big free-agent contracts with the Yankees in 1975, but he never changed a bit. He was a country farm boy from North Carolina, youngest of ten children. Real down-to-earth and easygoing. Forget the money, he was happiest just shooting the breeze with the ballpark grounds crew. Cat was grateful for the money, but he never apologized for it because he'd first had some bad dealings with Charlie Finley in Oakland, where Finley didn't pay up something Cat was supposed to get, and that's why he became a free agent. I remember after George Steinbrenner signed him to that huge contract, someone asked Cat what it meant for the future of baseball. He said, "I think the owners will start reading their contracts better."

Cat was a great team player, and would've fit right in

with the Yankee teams I played on; none of us got too big for his britches. Even Casey Stengel, as cold and tough as he could be, was never one to take the credit. In a way he's like Joe Torre, who cares for and respects his players, and they know it. Both became managers of the Yankees when nobody in the world wanted them; they even got ridiculed when they were hired—that's a lesson in humility you don't forget.

It's true many players today are too showy and selfish. I hear a lot of nostalgia for "when it was a game," but I do see some good signs of humility in baseball. Especially in how the players responded after 9/11—they really showed how insignificant they are and that they can do good things for people. Some of them, like Mike Piazza and Al Leiter of the Mets, I think they became more respected for their humility and for helping the victims' families.

Success spoils, but it doesn't have to. The players I like are the ones who know how to still be who they are. One of them is Luis Gonzalez of Arizona, a great kid even though he got the winning hit to beat us in the World Series in 2001. He was shy and skinny when he came up with Houston, when I was coaching there. I told him to use a heavier bat, because I thought it'd help and it did; he's become a darned good player.

If you have no humility, you don't know what you're missing. Everyone needs some advice, some more knowledge. I'm glad Bill Dickey took time to help me when I started out as an awful catcher. He taught me a lot about catching, and baseball taught me how to behave with decency, how to win and lose with grace, how to be grateful for whatever I have. I owe everything to baseball, and I never thought baseball owed me a thing. That's what I mean about learning humility.

"I Really Didn't Say Everything I Said."

A lot of people have put some funny words in my mouth.

I guess it started with my best friend Joe Garagiola on The Hill back home, but people just like telling stories about things I've said or didn't say. People imagine I'm some kind of wise guy or something. It never bothered me, and I always figured people should use their imaginations as much as they want, as long as it makes them happy.

I don't mean you should waste your imagination by daydreaming or hallucinating, but imagining things the way you want can only help you get it. Just think of what you want and figure out how to get it.

Kids need to use their imaginations, to be more creative, to play and make up games like we did in our day. We played everything—baseball, soccer, roller hockey, football, corkball, even a game called Indian Rubber, a kind of softball we played on the street. We used to hit bottle caps with broomsticks—that's great for your eye-hand coordination. We didn't have organized teams, just ourselves, our dreams and imaginations.

Me and Joe Garagiola, who grew up right across the street from me on Elizabeth Avenue, always dreamed we would become major-leaguers. We imagined we'd play for the St. Louis Browns or Cardinals, which Joe eventually did. We'd go to some of the games when we were kids, but it was more fun playing ball than watching it. Whenever Joe and I could smell a game starting up, we'd be there. Baseball was what I liked best, and that's all I imagined doing. When you talk, eat, sleep, and think one thing, that's what you ought to do.

Baseball as it's played now hasn't really changed. It still captures people's attention; great players and great teams do that. You never saw Babe Ruth on TV because there was none, but you heard and read about his home runs, how he visited sick kids in the hospitals, how he was real flamboyant, so he was easy for everyone to imagine. The Gas House Gang—the Cardinals teams in the 1930s—they dominated everyone's imagination in St. Louis back then. It was the Depression, but they were a colorful and scrappy bunch. Of course radio—which is all we had back then—helped your imagination. The game came to you in words, and you had to imagine what it all looked like. You saw these guys play and do everything, but it was in your head.

I think the Yankees today capture people's imagination

with the way they play—as a real team. No showboating, no nonsense, just playing hard and being professional. Cal Ripken was another guy who sort of captured people's imagination the way he played—especially when people were down on baseball after the strike. He reminded them of the honesty and the purity of the game, like everyone always imagined it.

I don't think you can live in a dream world, but it's fun to imagine certain guys in different eras. I once told Roger Clemens he could've played on our Yankee teams, meaning he's serious and intense and burns to win; I think he appreciated it. When I was with the Yankees, all we thought of was winning—we couldn't imagine losing. That becomes a habit and we had it—that feeling rubbed off on every player.

Every ballplayer, every successful person, has great imagination. They imagine themselves succeeding. Jack Nicklaus, well, he had a great mental game. He saw his golf shots before he hit them. Like I say, that's great imagination.

Dreaming is one thing, giving it focus is another. You have to realize how to realize your dream, as dumb as that sounds. Figure out how to improve, how to get help. Watching highlights on ESPN won't make you a better player; it's like playing the Lotto and dreaming of winning—it's probably not going to happen. Think positive, but think real, too.

That doesn't mean you shouldn't dream or imagine big things. It was only a movie, but *Field of Dreams* had a good message about baseball and life. The Kevin Costner character was trying to reconnect with his father because "he must have had dreams but he never did anything about them." Now Shoeless Joe Jackson coming out of the cornfields was another story—that's hard to imagine. But I tell any kid, there's no shame in trying your hardest to live your dream and coming up short. All you can do is give it your best shot; it's the only thing you have any control over.

Derek Jeter told his parents when he was eight years old he was going to play for the Yankees. That's what he imagined, then he worked hard, and got to live his dream. If he hadn't, I bet he'd still be successful in something else. People ask me a lot what would've happened if I never got to play baseball. Who knows? I never imagined anything but.

"Why Be **Jealous** over Things
You Don't Have?"

I don't think jealousy is too healthy, because it's a waste of time and it gets you nowhere. Being jealous of someone's success may be a natural feeling, but it's really foolishness; if some lazybones makes more at his job than you, how is getting angry and jealous going to help you?

Being around baseball I see a lot of jealousy. Mostly people are envious of the players' huge salaries today. Whenever someone asks if I'm jealous of the money these guys are making, I say heck no, I don't begrudge them at all. If some owner was willing to pay me millions, I'd have taken it, too. Who wouldn't? The owners are the ones who started it. Of course the salaries are kind of out of whack, but like I say, who would turn down a chance to be paid $10 million a year to play a kid's game?

Jealousy is kind of a negative action. When Texas paid Alex Rodriguez that $252 million, a lot of people got angry, or maybe just jealous that they don't have his talent. Even some players on other teams got jealous, but what good is that? Unless it makes you play better, why bother yourself over somebody else's money? It's like with movie stars—nobody gets mad when they get paid a lot. Besides, the market allows ballplayers to make the millions of dollars they make because people want to be entertained. They're paid well to do their job, and they're paid by owners who make more than anybody.

Being part of the Yankees for so long, I know other teams and fans can often get jealous. We win an awful lot and they don't. Too bad. When they complain that the Yankees have more money to build winners, that's not the whole truth—other teams have money, they just don't spend it right. The Yankees spend it better, putting it back into the team, the farm system, and the players. Plus winning creates its own motivation. I remember when the Yankees were giving out their 1998 championship rings the next season, and the players were real excited. Roger Clemens, who was new on the team, just stared and watched; he said it made him even hungrier to get one himself.

I always say these Yankees remind me of our teams a lot because we never had any jealousies; we all pulled for each other, no matter what. All of us loved Mickey Mantle because he was the best teammate you could have—we always tried to do things to help each other. I used to kid him that outfielders ought to pay their way into the ballpark, because it's so easy to play out there. And I used to tell him he was the worst outfielder we ever had. But when I started playing the outfield, I took it seriously and always asked him what he thought, and he was always real honest, especially if I made a mistake. I always say the best example of Mickey never being jealous was when he got hurt in 1961 and fell behind Roger Maris in the home run race. He led the cheers for Roger, because that's the way we all were. We didn't care who hit the homers, as long as we won.

I think a lot of jealousies in baseball are made up by the media. They make for good stories, or they would if they were true. You heard stories about Fred Lynn and Jim Rice in Boston, that they were each jealous of the attention the other one got, probably because their personalities were different. But they were really friends, and they respected and supported each other. When I was manager of the Yankees in 1984, Dave Winfield and Don Mattingly battled for the batting crown, and a lot of the writers said they didn't like each other—supposedly Winfield was jealous because Mattingly was more popular. That was a lot of baloney; they both wanted to win, both were good teammates, and both cheered each other's success. Believe me, there was no jealousy.

I think jealousy can turn to bitterness, and even worse. It's not something I understand, though I guess I'd understand it if my three older brothers got jealous because I was the only one who got the opportunity to do what I really wanted—to play baseball. Tony, Mike, and John were all excellent players and Tony—we called him Lefty—was the best in the family. But Pop never let them pursue baseball because he didn't see any future in it. Besides, my brothers had jobs that brought money to the house every week, and every penny counted. My brothers lobbied Pop to allow me the chance—they even offered to work extra to bring home more money to make up for me—and he finally agreed. When I made it to the Yankees years later, I told Pop he would've been a millionaire if he'd let my brothers play, too. He said, "Blame your mother."

With me and my brothers, it's a lot like it is with Frank and Joe Torre and how they treat each other—with pride, love, and support. Maybe not all siblings are like that, I don't know. Like in that women's baseball movie, *A League of Their Own,* where the younger sister is real jealous of her older sister, played by Geena Davis. Then she turned the jealousy into a positive because the competition brought out the best in her. It's nice when things can work out like that, but that was just a movie—more often than not, jealousy just gets in your way.

"Little League Is Good Because It Keeps Parents Off the Street and the **Kids** Out of the House."

As kids, we lived for sports. We played every game there was, even invented new ones. We had fun. We had spontaneity. We were carefree. We weren't forced to concentrate on just one thing—every season we'd play something new. We had no adults chauffeuring and scheduling and telling us what to do. It was a different time then, I guess. Now there's so much organizing and structuring what kids do—I don't think that always helps let kids be kids.

Kids should enjoy and get the most out of their childhoods. It shapes you, because you learn a lot about yourself. You learn your interests, you compare yourself with your peers, you make rules, you work things out yourself. Some things I learned as a kid, I still draw from today. I think I got my stubbornness as a young kid. But I also got determination and the ability to get along with others. You never felt the pressures some of these kids today have. I think that's why a lot of them drop out of sports when they get to twelve or thirteen—it's not fun anymore.

Baseball is a real constant in our country, though it's different for kids. The sandlot pickup games in the neighborhood seem a thing of the past. Heck, we'd play all day long on the street or playground, sunrise to dark, no umpires, no uniforms, no rules, we'd just play. Like I say, today everything's adult-structured, and kids don't just play among themselves that much. Back then you'd knock on a few doors, and you had a ballgame on the street. Now you have to arrange appointments to play. Parents schedule "play dates"; it's not real informal.

I'd like to see more kids fend for themselves. Find ways to play because it's better being out in fresh air than inside. Plus it's a good outlet and keeps you out of trouble. At least it did for us on The Hill, where we played all summer with patchwork equipment—nailed bats and taped-together baseballs—then turned to soccer in winter. Playing, you develop strengths you didn't know you had. Plus we were training all the time, not knowing we were training, but we were. I know soccer helped my agility, and I'm sure hitting bottlecaps with broomsticks helped my hand-eye coordination.

We had fun as kids, just ask Joe Garagiola or anybody in our neighborhood. It gave us a lot of joy and freedom and self-reliance. People think I tutored my sons into being ballplayers—no way. I barely played with them because I wasn't there that much. When I'd come home and they'd ask to play, I'd tell them that's what they had brothers for. And Larry, Tim, and Dale used to play all the time with their friends or make up games themselves, no parental interference.

When we weren't playing ball, we hung out at Riva's Candy Store, or our gang's clubhouse, which was an old garage and cost us twelve cents a month. Like any kids, we had our own moneymaking enterprises so we could go to the movies: We'd shovel manure or buy boxes of cigarettes and candy bars wholesale then sell them for a tiny profit. As kids we had fun and we knew right from wrong because we went to church a lot, which is what you did on The Hill.

Truth is, I think kids are pretty honest people. They have good instincts, they basically know right from wrong, who's good or who's rotten. If you were a kid growing up in the Depression, usually a baseball player was your hero. Mine was Joe Medwick, a wild-swinging slugger for the Cardinals. He was my customer when I sold newspapers on Southwest and Kings Highway. He'd give me a nickel for a three-cent paper, and always stop and shoot the breeze for a couple of minutes. Years later when I was a rookie in spring training with the Yankees, he showed me some outfield techniques, too.

Baseball gave us a happy childhood. As kids, we believed that professional athletes like Joe Medwick were good people who wanted to play sports because they loved playing, not just because they loved getting money, because they didn't make that much. Baseball to us was a kid's game; I think it still is and always will be. I also think we're all kids when it comes to sports, especially baseball.

Even today I kind of call everybody "kid," including guys who are older than me. Hank Bauer thinks I'm nuts when I call him that. I regard the Yankee players today as kids. The Brooklyn Dodgers became the "Boys of Summer." The Phillies in 1950 were called the "Whiz Kids." Two of the greatest players ever were The Kid (Ted Williams) and the Say Hey Kid (Willie Mays).

Baseball brought out the kid in you, and it still does. I felt real lucky to play a kid's game for a living—I always say it beat working. To me it's a game forever connected to childhood, no matter what generation, no matter what else is popular. It was always fun. That's the biggest thing I can hope for kids: Just let them go out and play and have fun.

"**Little** Things Are Big."

Doing the little things can make a big difference. It doesn't matter whether you're working around the house or playing baseball, there's always a right way and a wrong way, and it's the little details that mean a lot. Paying attention to the basics—in baseball, it's the fundamentals— is a little thing that's a big thing.

You always hear about not sweating the small stuff. Well, some little things they say you shouldn't worry about are more important than the big stuff. It's better to never assume anything.

I was real lucky to play for Casey Stengel, who was a stickler for fundamentals, and we practiced them all the time. Casey used to say that most games are lost, not won, meaning that when you mess up the little fundamentals— making a cutoff play, advancing a runner when making an out—you're not going to win. Our teams weren't speed burners, but no team went from first to third better than us. I'll tell you, Casey was great with young players, too, because he liked teaching them all the little stuff that was important. He actually started the instructional league (he called it the "instructural" league) to help rookies; he knew that making them know the little things would give us an advantage.

It's true in anything. I was a big football fan, and I got to know Vince Lombardi when he was an assistant with the New York Giants, and believe me, he was real big on drills, details, and discipline. When he got to Green Bay he'd run that sweep fifty times in practice, and he'd go over the little things over and over each time, the things that made it work. Another great teacher was John Wooden, the basketball coach at UCLA. He didn't believe in marathon practices, but he never missed the littlest things. I heard he even lectured his players on the right way to put on their socks because he felt sore feet would hurt their performance.

To me baseball is the truest game of little things: a pitcher tipping off his pitches; going to a lighter bat when you get a bit older; a foul tip that gives you another life, like in Game 7 of the 1956 World Series when Don Newcombe almost struck me out, but my foul tip popped out of Roy Campanella's mitt; I hit a home run on the next pitch and we went on to win.

Truth is, our Yankee teams didn't usually bash the other teams with homers—we usually won by doing all the little things. Nobody bunted and hit behind the runner better than Phil Rizzuto. You can't teach power and speed, but you can teach hustling and proper technique. Our pitchers were good at the little things, too—working fast, getting ahead of the count, ruining a batter's rhythm.

Everybody made a big to-do about Derek Jeter's running cutoff play in the 2001 playoffs against Oakland—when he got the ball in foul territory on the throw to the plate and flipped it to Posada to catch Jeremy Giambi—but to me it was really a little thing. He was being mentally sharp, making himself useful when the play wasn't directed at him—Jeter always does those little things real good. Funny, people asked if I'd ever seen anything like it, and I had: Casey used to have us practice all different cutoff plays all the time. (And another kind of little thing at work on that play was on the Oakland side, when Giambi didn't slide; that was a little thing that combined with Jeter's little thing to make the difference between winning and losing.)

These Yankees appreciate the importance of little things, because the manager and coaches preach it. And the players play smart. Sure, they've got good talent and good pitchers, but they maybe do the little things better than anyone—like drawing pitchers into high pitch counts, moving runners over, covering all the basics.

I'm big on little things when I watch movies, especially the baseball ones. *Eight Men Out*—about the 1919 Black Sox scandal—was one of the best because of all the details. Everything looked and felt real: the uniforms, the ballpark, the players. They even had Shoeless Joe Jackson batting lefty, which was correct, not like the guy in *Field of Dreams* who played him batting righty. It's a little thing, but it sticks in your mind.

Baseball is mostly a head game. It's all about making the right decisions. Same thing in life—make the right decisions, take care of the little things. Like I say, you can observe a lot by watching—and you learn a lot, too. Little things like being on time, being prepared for bad weather, saying please and thank you to people you don't know, and never taking anything for granted because you just never know. Maybe that's small stuff, but it sounds to me like it's worth sweating over.

M

"We Made Too Many Wrong **Mistakes**."

Life is a learning experience, only if you learn. That's why a mature person gets a little better, a little wiser, with experience. He makes a mistake, but he can face up to it, deal with it, and help solve the problems he may have caused. But an immature person doesn't get it. When things go bad, he'll act worse. He'll blame others, get too emotional, and even avoid the problem.

Baseball's the same way—guys either learn from their experience, or they stay immature. You see it with pitchers all the time. I'm supposed to have said that all pitchers are crybabies or liars. That's not true; I never said it, and not all of them are. But I've seen enough pitchers to tell you they're a different breed. They're the most alone players on the field, and everything depends on them. They can fool you or they can fool themselves and they can drive you crazy. But you can't give up on them too easily, because in a year they can become a completely different pitcher.

The ones who find maturity can find greatness. On the Yankees, we had some late bloomers, Allie Reynolds especially. People forget that the Cleveland Indians called him up during World War II to replace Bob Feller, who was in the Army. But Reynolds was pretty wild, and got a reputation as someone who couldn't handle pressure—a choker. When the Yankees got him, he changed; he listened and he learned. He matured. It wasn't until he was in his midthirties that he became a great pitcher. As he said, "You get smart only when you begin getting old."

Like I say, immature people often avoid their problems and don't learn from their mistakes. On sheer talent, one of the best I ever saw was Joe Pepitone, who I managed in 1964. But Pepi was a real wisecracker and always found trouble. I got him to play almost every game that season, although he always said he felt sick and begged not to play. Honestly, I don't think he took his career seriously enough. He never really matured and realized the potential he had.

When you hear someone say, "Grow up," that's what they mean. Take responsibility. Learn from your failures and successes. Maturity is a physical thing, but also an emotional thing. My success in baseball was because of maturity. You can't teach experience, but I always say that Bill Dickey learned me his. I was a lousy catcher my first couple of years—all I really cared about was hitting. But the

Yankees brought Dickey in to help me in 1949, and he worked me some long hours. Mainly he worked on my mechanics and my confidence. Dickey definitely awakened my pride, and I became a better player, a more mature one.

I think how you handle frustration is an important sign of maturity. Everybody gets frustrated, who doesn't? Who hasn't kicked the ground or gotten really mad? Once I threw a pack of cigarettes at George Steinbrenner—not one of my better moments. But cursing your fate and blowing up isn't the way to change things. The best thing is to use anger as a source of energy. Getting mad at the club's owner can make you try doubly hard to prove him wrong. Of course it's pretty hard getting any boss to admit he's wrong.

Back to pitchers. When I was coaching with the Mets in the 1960s, we had Nolan Ryan. He was a baby—not a crybaby, but just real young and immature. He could throw the heck out of the ball, but whenever he couldn't get it over he'd just throw it harder and get wilder. He also had trouble fitting in in New York and he got frustrated—I remember he was even thinking of quitting baseball for good. But when Nolan got traded to the Angels in 1972, everything turned around.

The big thing is, he matured. He listened to his pitching coach, Tom Morgan, who was a good, calm pitcher for us in the early 1950s. "Plowboy"—that's what we called Morgan because he stooped when he walked—told Nolan he didn't have to throw every pitch 100 mph. Nolan worked hard and developed a great workout ethic. He grew up as a pitcher and as a person. Honestly, when I was a coach with the Astros in the late 1980s, Nolan was still throwing the ball as hard as he did twenty years earlier.

When you see Randy Johnson, you see another Nolan Ryan—he was also wild, frustrated, emotional, immature, but Nolan had a talk with him at some point and things turned around. I guess that's a sign of maturity, too. It's learning from others. It's being confident enough yourself to get what you want, or you'll never get it.

Accepting frustration and owning up to mistakes is important, too. In baseball there's guys who won't talk to the media after they have a bad game, which really isn't too mature. That was never a problem for Bob Feller, who was already pretty grown up at seventeen when he first pitched in the majors. Not that it happened much, but he always said that if you gave up a game-winning home run, it was a test of maturity to stand in front of your locker fifteen minutes later and talk about it to the world. Because, he asked, how many people in other professions would be willing to have their job performance analyzed in front of millions?

"It's So Crowded, **Nobody** Goes There."

Lots of people say New York is the greatest city in the world, because it is. It's a pretty no-nonsense place, too, because people aren't shy about telling you what they think. When you rub elbows with ten million people, there's a lot of aggressiveness going on. But competition always brings out the best, and New York has the best theater, the best restaurants, the best museums, the best diversity anywhere.

I consider myself a New Yorker, even though I grew up in St. Louis and live in New Jersey. I spent forty years in baseball in New York and, like a lot of people, it's where you get established in life that sticks with you. When I was manager of the Yankees in 1964 (and later with the Mets) and then got fired, I could have gone to work in other cities, but I stayed because I loved New York.

When I was a rookie with the Yankees in 1947, I lived in the Edison Hotel in midtown. I found that if you can't find something to do in New York, you're probably ill. For a twenty-two-year-old kid, it was pretty intimidating, all those skyscrapers and throngs of people. Even today it's still kind of overwhelming, especially if you're looking for parking.

After we got married in 1949, Carm and I moved to Gerard Avenue in the Bronx, just a couple of blocks from Yankee Stadium. Everything you needed was real close and there was a small-town feel in the neighborhood, everybody was friendly. This was after World War II, and there was a real baseball fever in the city—people know and love their baseball in New York like nowhere else. There were three teams—us, the Dodgers, and the Giants, and a dozen newspapers in the city then. All the bakeries and butcher shops had radios with a game on—you felt baseball everywhere.

No place gets wrapped up in baseball like New York. When I was a coach on the Mets in 1969, the city had a carnival atmosphere and it really lifted everybody's spirits. We were such underdogs, I think we gave people reason to believe they could realize their dreams, that they could make it in New York, too.

New York's changed over the years. There's no more Toots Shor's, which was a great hangout, or the old Madison Square Garden on 50th Street, where I used to always go see hockey and the fights. Times Square's real different, except that there's still neon signs everywhere, and a lot of energy on the street.

But New York is still the truest melting pot—nowhere else do you have so many different races and ethnic groups.

And they're not here as tourists, they actually live here. It's still a place you come to for opportunity and for a new life, and that's the way it's always been. My father came a century ago from the Old Country, because the farming in his village in northern Italy wasn't so good anymore. Pop was alone when he left home, figuring he'd better save up a little money before sending for my mom. He didn't settle in New York—he worked in Colorado and California as a farmhand before settling in St. Louis—but he told me that the first place he came to was Ellis Island, and that kind of inspired him.

One thing about the city is it can be kind of gruff. You get judged pretty quick. People have an edge; if you're looking for politeness, it may not be your place. Everything is always fast-paced and hectic and "in a New York minute." That means you do things in a hurry, but I always have to ask, What's the hurry?

New York does get a bad rap sometimes. It ain't cheap, that's for sure. You get some unruly people, but you get them everywhere. I think the fans, especially in baseball, get a bad rap because I've seen fans in other cities and New Yorkers are the most passionate—they know baseball and they let you know when you mess up. But unlike other places, they'll appreciate the other guy for a good performance—they're great fans. That's what I told Jason Giambi when he was thinking of signing with the Yankees: If you do good here, there's nowhere in the world better to play. I told him he could make a lot of money off the field, too.

New York City always makes you feel like you're part of something big. It's full of excitement and history—that's why Yankee Stadium is so special. It's like a great cathedral, bigger than life, just a legendary place. I'll always remember my first World Series in 1947, beating the Brooklyn Dodgers—the level of excitement was hard to describe. We had over seventy-three thousand people at the first game and the game was broadcast over Armed Forces Radio around the world. Television was still new, but it really felt like the whole world was watching. Joe DiMaggio told me that was the most exciting World Series he ever played in, and I think it was spiced because of our archrivals in Brooklyn.

When we won, the Yankees threw a lavish party in the Biltmore Hilton, then we got a ticker-tape parade in the Canyon of Heroes. That felt great, too, being part of a New York tradition that started in the 1880s when they had one for the Statue of Liberty. Carm worked on the committee to restore the statue, so she knows all that history stuff.

There's been a lot said about New York since what happened on 9/11. It's made everyone think about the world and how everything has changed. Nobody will forget that tragedy, or the people who lost their lives. I think New York City is kind of an emblem of America, because it's made up of so many different people, all trying to pull together. I was proud to see the Yankees and Mets players show the city's spirit by wearing the NYPD and NYFD caps in honor of the policemen and firemen, and dedicate themselves to helping out; they're New Yorkers and they care. When Mayor Giuliani asked me to do a commercial to help promote New York City for tourism after the tragedy, it was the very least I could do. Of course the city was already on the mend, because that's the beauty of New York: Like someone said, "It's the greatest city in the world—you got a problem with that?"

"It Was a Once-in-a-Lifetime **Opportunity**, and I've Had a Couple of Those."

When you hear that America is a place of opportunity, it's true. There are plenty of things anybody can be if they work hard enough—and they're given the chance. Heck, look at all the ballplayers in the big leagues today; they come from everywhere—from South America to Japan and even beyond. They all got an opportunity to show what they could do and they did it. Most everybody in life gets a chance to prove themselves at something, and usually you get more than one chance. But it's better to do better the second time, or you'll soon be running out of chances.

I feel fortunate for my opportunity—me, a kid from The Hill, the son of immigrants, who quit school but got a chance to play baseball. That's the great thing about this game—poor boy, rich boy, they're all on equal footing in professional baseball. What counts is ability and only that.

I don't agree when someone says something is a "once-in-a-lifetime opportunity." How do they know? Why only once? Maybe sales guys are trained to say that, I don't know; we always hear that stuff, "now for a limited time only" or "don't let this opportunity pass you by," but that's just salesmen talk. Opportunities can happen out of the blue. Sometimes it's hard to recognize an opportunity or where it will lead, but if you make the most of whatever you're doing, and if opportunity comes and you're ready, maybe you'll get lucky.

Playing American Legion baseball as a teenager was a great opportunity for me. I didn't make any money, but it was a tremendous experience. It was my first organized team—Stockham Post—and I got my first actual uniform, got to travel and meet different people, got to test my skills against real good players, and I also got a break because our manager was Leo Browne, who loved baseball and liked me. He arranged for me and Joe Garagiola to try out for the St. Louis Cardinals in Sportsman's Park when we were sixteen. Joe got a $500 signing bonus, and I got nothing, just Branch Rickey telling me that I'd never be a big-league ballplayer. A year later, after the 1942 World Series, Browne called his friend John Schulte, who was a coach for the Yankees and lived in St. Louis. He told Schulte I was worth the $500, so the Yankees signed me.

When opportunity knocks, you got to answer—especially in baseball, which is a game of opportunities and missed opportunities. It can rip your heart out and then make you as happy as a clam. I think the biggest regrets in life are missed opportunities, but you can't get pessimistic over things that should've been or you'll just go into a depression.

One of the worst things I ever felt was back in 1951 when Allie Reynolds was working on a no-hitter in the ninth inning. We got two outs, then needed to get Ted Williams, only the greatest hitter in the game, for the final out. Ted hit a high twisting pop behind the plate and I circled under the ball, and then put my glove up—and the ball dropped out. I felt terrible. And it didn't feel so good either when Reynolds accidentally stepped on my hand as I fell down. Allie said, OK, let's try it again, and when I got to the plate Williams started giving me grief. "You really put me in a hell of a spot," he said. "What am I supposed to do now? I get a base hit and I'm a bad guy."

Luckily he popped up the very next pitch, in nearly the same area, and this time I caught it. You'd think I was the hero, the way my teammates jumped all over me. I got another opportunity, a chance for redemption, and that's all you can hope for. What are the odds of getting that same opportunity? I don't know, but to me failure is just an opportunity to start again. Whenever there's a window of opportunity, use it. Like I said, negatives can be opportunities, too. Getting fired from a job may be a good opportunity, because it's a chance to start fresh and get a better job— that's the only way to look at it.

Illness, too, can be a good opportunity because it can

help you make good changes. After I got a physical about ten years ago, my doctor was concerned about my irregular heartbeat and stamina. That's when I quit smoking and my condition now is great—at least, I feel pretty good.

Opportunities are always going to be out there, no matter what you do. You always hear about career opportunities and golden opportunities and photo opportunities (when did taking pictures become a photo opportunity?). And now they talk about "save opportunities" in baseball—they didn't have that when we played. They didn't even count saves. Now when relief pitchers come in, they either get a save or they don't. And if they screw up a lot, they may have to find another career opportunity.

"If the World Were **Perfect**,
It Wouldn't Be."

You have to take the good with the bad, because it's not a perfect world. It's OK to strive for perfection, but there's a downside to always trying to get things perfect. Too often you get frazzled and frustrated when things don't turn out the way you want, even getting stressed and self-destructive. I've seen lots of perfectionists, guys like Mickey Mantle, have too high expectations for themselves; Mickey would explode when he didn't hit a home run every time up, and Casey Stengel would have to remind him that the poor water cooler wasn't striking him out.

To be great in anything, you have to have some perfectionist qualities. Mickey had tremendous desire and intensity, and if he'd had two good legs, he might have been the best player ever. I always said Paul O'Neill reminded me a lot of Mickey, because he was pretty darn hard on himself, too. He had a fierceness about him because he was such a perfectionist, and it ate at him something bad when he didn't play like he wanted to play. Luckily, the Yankees have switched to plastic coolers. But you see how perfectionists can be too demanding, as intense and high-strung as a thoroughbred; it happens in the big leagues and even in the little leagues. Everybody wants to win or go four for four, but sometimes you don't. That's when we say, Get a grip.

Don't get me wrong: Aiming for excellence, being a perfectionist, is part of what makes great players great. Tiger Woods is a perfectionist, but he's also a realist. He's always tinkering with his swing, making adjustments to a real difficult game. When he was younger he'd show his temper, but he doesn't have a lot of meltdowns anymore, mostly because he usually wins, but also because he's comfortable in knowing he gave it his best. DiMaggio was like that too, and he was the closest thing to a perfect ballplayer I ever saw. He wanted to be the best, and he expected his teammates to be their best, too. He was like Jackie Robinson in that he expected the same out of others as he got out of himself.

Ted Williams was a lot like Joe, but more as a hitting perfectionist. He always said he wanted to be remembered as the greatest hitter who ever lived. Not everybody is going to be the greatest something ever, but it's important to find something you really love and do it as well as you can. You don't have to be a perfectionist. You can strive for good health, a long life, and make things better for others along the way. That was the good thing about Ted when his hitting days were over—he's had a great life.

What is perfection anyway? If perfect 10s for those gymnasts and skaters are real perfection, I don't know. It's not something they really control—it kind of depends on the opinions of others, and some of those Olympic judges make you wonder.

Of all the sports, baseball is the closest thing to perfect. The bases are ninety feet apart and that's a pretty perfect distance. Think about all the close plays: There's one batter, one pitcher, three outs, nine innings—same as it's been for over a hundred years. Yet you can't honestly expect perfection in baseball because the best players fail seven out of ten times at the plate. And even the best pitchers get knocked out of games early.

Once in a long while, a pitcher will pitch a perfect game—twenty-seven batters up, twenty-seven down. No question, catching Don Larsen's perfect game in the 1956 World Series was one of my greatest thrills. He was perfect; pitching is about control and that day Larsen's was the best it ever was. Of course, he isn't perfect if Mickey doesn't chase down Gil Hodges's shot to left-center in the fifth. Or Gil McDougald doesn't make a great play in the seventh.

But the greatest thing about Larsen's performance was the timing. He got knocked out of Game 2 of the Series. He was a bit down on himself, and who knew if he'd even pitch anymore in the Series. He wasn't a star, either; he had lost

21 games a couple of years earlier, and he had a reputation for enjoying nightlife—we used to call him Gooney Bird. But Larsen was perfect for one day in the perfect place—Yankee Stadium—and at the perfect time—the World Series. Except for something like world peace breaking out, nothing was ever more perfect than that.

"If You Ask Me a **Question** I Don't Know,
I'm Not Going to Answer."

What is the meaning of life? How do you think the Yankees will do? How the heck am I supposed to know? People ask me questions all the time—good ones, dumb ones, ones I just can't answer. Sometimes there's no right or wrong answer, so I just say I don't know. That's always the best policy. When you make things up people will know you're a phony and won't trust you.

When I was managing with the Yankees and the Mets, I always tried to answer every sportswriter's question as honestly as I could. That was their job, to ask, and it was part of mine to give answers. It did get hard at times, especially after a tough game. Sometimes you just don't feel like talking. Sometimes I'd tell the writers that if they asked me a question I don't know, I'm not going to answer. Or I'd tell them I wish I had an answer because I'm tired of answering that question.

I wasn't trying to be a smart aleck or make their jobs harder; I was just being honest. Everybody has to answer questions every day. If you're a public figure, like a ballplayer or a manager or a politician, you have a responsibility to answer questions, because in a way the public is paying you. But I think it's important to know who's questioning you. What's their agenda? What exactly do they want to know? Who wants to know? I never give long answers—that's just me.

Sometimes I have a habit of answering a question with a question. Every now and then someone asks me what time is it, and I say, "Now?" Or if someone asks me why I'm wearing something, I'll say, "Why are you wearing *that?*" Or I'll ask a question before someone asks me. There must've been a hundred newspaper reporters and photographers who streamed into the locker room after Don Larsen pitched his perfect game in the 1956 World Series, and somebody said I just asked them, "What's new?"

Asking good questions isn't easy. Believe me, I've heard some doozies. Like the guy who asked Casey Stengel after Larsen's perfect game, "Is this the best game he ever pitched?" I can't remember Casey's answer, but I can't forget that question.

When I'm being interviewed or talking to reporters, I don't say much—what else can I say? I don't like talking about personal stuff. When I signed my 1958 contract, it was for a cut in salary—my first bad year after ten good ones. I wasn't real happy about it, but the reporters kept pressing me with questions: Was it this much? Less than that much? More than this much? I was going along with it until I realized they were trying to pin me down, so I stopped answering. I'm not crazy about nosy questions—who is?

I admit I wasn't a scholar in the classroom or liked answering any questions as a kid. Once when someone asked me how I liked school, I replied, "Closed." But I will say that learning really takes place with questions, because it answers curiosity or the need to know and decide things. And good questions can get you the information you need.

Like if I'm buying a car, I'll leave my wallet home the first time and just ask questions. What are the payments? What kind of warranty? What's the downside of the car? The right questions can help you make the right decisions.

I will say that I'm asked a lot of questions, and it's not always my idea of fun, especially those wide-open questions. Like whenever I'm asked, "What was it like to play for the Yankees?" I just say, "It was great." Not a great answer, but not a great question, either.

I don't mind good questions, especially if they make you think. Kids at our museum like to ask a lot of questions, and that's good. Some are dandies, like the time a nine-year-old kid on a school trip asked me, "If you were alive today, would you beat Mark McGwire in home runs?"

To be honest, I'm surprised people want to interview me, because I don't think I always answer real well. People remind me of the time a radio interviewer tried to switch things by playing word association. Instead of asking me questions, he'd say a name, and I had to give an immediate impression. So he started by saying, "Mickey Mantle," and I replied, "What about him?"

"Congratulations—I Knew the **Record** Would Stand Until It Was Broken."

I don't know if respect is going out of fashion, but sometimes it's not so popular. Look at some of your older people, sometimes they get treated pretty rude. Look at political campaigns—try to remember the last one that wasn't nasty or negative. Even in sports now, guys talk junk or waggle their fingers or strut around like roosters. Where'd the respect go? I don't know.

We were always taught to be gracious winners and graceful losers, and to respect authority—especially your parents. Especially when they ask or expect you to do something. When I was a kid growing up, Pop always expected that beer on the table when he came home every day from the brickyard. If it wasn't, you'd get a big thwack from his hand. If Pop told you something, you'd better respect it.

Pop was from the Old World, and that's how they did it

in those days—by fear. Just like those old football coaches—they'd intimidate you. Now it's different. To get respect you have to give it. You hear guys called "players' coaches" and "players' managers," which I think means that the players respect their boss because he respects them. As a manager, I never humiliated a player or talked about him to the press—if I had a problem with him, I'd call him aside. Joe Torre's great at that, because he's a straight shooter who respects his players and they respect him. The way Joe carries himself, it carries down to the players.

I don't think fear breeds respect like it used to. Being firm, genuine, and considerate does. Not that you have to go around always saying, "Mister" or "Madam" or "Sir"—that can be too formal or stiff. I know Derek Jeter always says "Mr. Torre," but that's just his way of showing respect. And he means it.

How do you show respect? For one, look a person in the eye when you talk to him—that shows you're serious and you care. I always go by that Golden Rule: Treat others the way you'd like to be. I'd never turn around to argue a called pitch with an ump, because that's showing him up; I'd just ask him, where was it? I respected most umps, even the ones I gave a hard time to. I remember a beef with Cal Hubbard, who I thought was missing some pitches. Then I got real angry over one and I began stomping and yelling. He told me to stop or he'd toss me; I told him if he'd admit missing the pitch, I'd stop yelling. He wouldn't and he ejected me. It was a bad scene—people threw garbage on the field and I got fined by the league. I felt sort of bad, so the next game, I went over to Hubbard to shake his hand, and I told him he shouldn't have taken me so seriously. I still respected him and vice versa. I think.

Respecting your opponent is big in Japan. When we played exhibitions there in the 1950s, if a pitcher hit you he'd come off the mound, take off his cap, and apologize. If you ever see karate, they bow before they start. I think it's their way of saying hello, and acknowledging they'll play fair. We never did that in baseball, but we sure as heck respected all our opponents, especially the Dodgers. They had great players over there—Jackie Robinson, Pee Wee Reese, Campy, Duke Snider, Gil Hodges—and we respected every one of them. You had to. They were our opponents, and opponents are the ones who want the same thing you want. Plus those guys all were pretty fierce competitors, and always handled themselves first-class. Pee Wee was a good leader, not a rah-rah kind, but just by his actions. He'd help Jackie, but Jackie won respect himself by the way he handled everything. Gil was great, too. Years later, he inherited me as a coach on the Mets in 1968, and he could've let me go, but instead he made me feel needed. Everyone respected him because of his integrity. Plus he brought discipline to the Mets, who were a bunch of kids then. If he gave you a glare, you'd sure know it.

Respect may have won us a game in the 1969 World

Series. Cleon Jones got hit on the foot with a pitch, only the umpire didn't see it. But Gil brought over the ball and he showed the ump the shoe polish on it, and they gave Jones first base—and then Donn Clendenon homered to get us back into a game we went on to win. Gil might have been showing any smudged ball to that ump, but I think the umps respected Gil too much to doubt him.

There's so much to respect in baseball. You have to respect the rules, the traditions, the history, the people dedicated to it. You play through injuries, play when you're tired—that's part of the bargain. When people ask me why I stayed away from Yankee Stadium for fourteen years, it was a matter of respect, or actually disrespect. George Steinbrenner didn't tell me face-to-face he was firing me as manager, he had someone else tell me. I'd been fired before, but at least the owner told me man to man. With George, that was a pretty big sign of disrespect and it kind of roiled in me for a while. But we eventually made peace when he sought me out and now that's all in the past.

One sport where they really get things right is in hockey. Those guys have so much respect for their sport that they won't even touch the Stanley Cup until they've earned the right to by winning the championship. I'm a hockey nut, and I really enjoy the handshakes at the end of the playoff series because it's what sports are all about. Those guys mash each other's heads in, but they have enough respect to look the other guy in the eye and say "Good job." The war's over but the respect's not over. It shows itself in the handshakes. It should be the same thing with games, records, accomplishments, whatever. You do good, someone else comes along and does better, you shake his hand and congratulate him and you can both feel good about what you've done.

"**Someone's** Got to Win and Someone's Got to Lose, and That Was Us."

Sportsmanship is such a big issue in youth leagues, high school, college, and the pros, and it makes me wonder: Why don't people get it? I blame a lot of the parents, because they forget about the good of the kids; they forget sports is supposed to be about enjoyment and fair competition. And a lot of adults lose it every day—especially their temper. They push their kids, yell too much at them and the umps, and get way too emotional. If you're a kid, this isn't what you're supposed to learn from sports.

Young kids are impressionable. Believe me, I was one once. And I always learned it was important to play hard, play well, and sit down. Win with grace, shake your opponent's hand, never do any show-up-the-other-guy stuff. When you lose, so what? Losing doesn't mean you're a loser; winning doesn't mean you're a winner. Someone's got to win and someone's got to lose. Just make sure you gave it your best.

I'll tell you, there's a big difference between losing and failure. That's where adults can make the difference. Show kids there's actually good in losing—like good effort, good improvement, and hopefully good motivation to do even better next time. Maybe you can't control winning or losing, but you control your effort and the way you act. As kids playing ball on The Hill, we didn't really care who won; we didn't have rumbles over close calls, we just chose up sides, played, and had fun. When I was twelve, I started playing baseball for the Stags A.C., a team that Joe Garagiola and I and other kids on The Hill started. We joined a league run by the YMCA, led by a great guy named Joe Causino, who used to always tell us: "Play hard, play clean, always listen to your mother, go to church on Sunday, and nothing bad is ever gonna happen to you." So that's what we did.

When I got to the major leagues, being a winner and winning was a big deal to the Yankees. That's the basic idea when you play—to win. But in all our years winning championships, even the five straight we won from 1949–53, we never got big-headed or beat our chests or disgraced anybody. I always felt we showed good sportsmanship; we always respected our opponent, and believe me we had some pretty fierce rivalries with the Brooklyn Dodgers in the World Series. But I'll always remember Jackie Robinson, Pee Wee Reese, and those guys coming into our clubhouse to congratulate us after we beat them. They were pretty down, so that showed class. When they finally beat us in 1955, a bunch of us went into their clubhouse and congratulated them. I wasn't real overjoyed, but someone's got to win and someone's got to lose and that was us. People think we hated them—not so. We were friends off the field, that's the way we all were.

Money and winning have changed things; the behavior by players and fans in the pros can get pretty bad. Bad tempers and too much posturing, it's all too much. I cringe whenever I see guys stand at home plate and admire their home runs, which only shows up the pitcher. If that happened in our day, you better believe you'd get a fastball buzzing your ear next time up.

Showing off and self-promotion, you see it in every sport. There's too much of that aren't-I-great nonsense. Too much attention on the individual over the team. That's why people really loved the sportsmanship between McGwire and Sosa during their home run race in 1998. It was friendly and serious competition, but they were hugging and smiling and cheering each other and it was genuine. They weren't only thinking of themselves.

Sports is a good test of how you act under pressure. As a player and manager, there were times I got pretty mad on the field, but not too often and not too much. Sure I'd disagree with or argue bad calls, but I never self-destructed; I had a responsibility to perform my best, respect the umpires and respect the opponent. That's what we always tell the kids in the sportsmanship program at our museum: If you don't respect your opponent, you'll never get respect yourself.

I think many athletes don't realize how much they're an example to kids, and that brings with it a responsibility, whether they like it or not. And fans have a responsibility, too. Heckling is as old as sports itself and it adds something to games—what it adds I'm not sure, but it's part of what people seem to like about going to the ballpark. I didn't mind getting ragged because it made me concentrate better. But sometimes spectators get out of hand and show bad sportsmanship when they cuss or chant obscene things—that happens too much, I think. I love the Yankee fans—they're the most knowledgeable in the world—but a few of them I'd rather see watch the games at home.

Some people think sportsmanship is dead or dying but I don't know; it's just that the media plays up a lot of bad stuff, especially some of those violent cases, like that hockey father who killed another father. But then on the other side there's the popularity of golf. People are discovering more and more that it's a great game with a lot of great qualities—fair play, honesty, discipline, and players call penalties on themselves (sometimes). It's a game made for sportsmanship. Well, there are some guys who should probably stop cheating on their handicaps—and they know who they are.

It would be nice if those shows like "SportsCenter" decided for a while that they're just going to show what players did, and not the whole reaction and celebration that follows from every tackle, every home run, every goal. Kids get the message that the way to be on TV is to make a spectacle of yourself, and they think that being on TV is what's important. If the guys showing football highlights would show the tackle but not the sack dance that followed, maybe we'd see fewer guys beating their chests and more guys giving their opponent a hand. Your opponent isn't your enemy; it's just a game, and sportsmanship ought to be a part of it again. Or am I dreaming?

"Pair Up in **Threes**."

Working with others to achieve something, I think, is the best experience you can have. It's a great feeling to win. It's even greater when you work together to get it . . . and share it.

One of my most prized things is a plaque from the Yankees with pictures of the twelve guys who were on the 1949–53 championship teams, the only club ever to win five straight championships. To me it's a symbol of teamwork.

It didn't matter if we had stars like DiMaggio, we were all pretty unselfish. So was Joe. Everything he did was for the team good. Nobody worried about what the other guy was making; all we worried about was our jobs, picking each other up, getting into the World Series. That was our job—getting into the World Series. Sure, guys had individual goals, but the team always came first. When Casey

Stengel was our manager, it was teamwork or the highway. He'd bench your butt if he thought it was best for the team, that's how it was. He started the platoon system, even before football did. And he'd tick off guys like Hank Bauer and Gene Woodling, who thought they should play more—that was their competitive nature. But you couldn't argue with the results.

I remember Casey once replaced Moose Skowron, who was batting cleanup one day in Detroit, for a pinch hitter—in the first inning! Moose was pretty steamed. I think he left the ballpark he was so mad. The next day Casey called him in and said, "I'm out to win a pennant and don't give a damn how you feel." That's the way it was—everybody had to put aside their egos. Casey just knitted all the pieces together, and everybody contributed for the team good.

I think we were a good model of teamwork, and you don't see it much today. Maybe the players change teams so much, I'm not sure. People blame the players for being greedy, but I blame the owners—they're the ones who want instant success, sudden gratification. They bring in hired guns like in those old Westerns, and often they don't fit too good. There's no teamwork or unselfishness. Like Casey used to say, "It's easy to get the players. Getting 'em to play together, that's the hard part."

I'm no business expert, but you don't have to be to figure out that Enron mess. Those guys confused getting rich with being successful. They had all these secret things going on. It wasn't the company's success that mattered, it was their own. You had honest people there, but they didn't stand a chance with all that individual glory going on.

It's no big secret you need teamwork in everything. That means you need trust. And you need a shared goal—no private agenda. That's the job of a baseball manager or a CEO—to make sure everyone's on the same page. If you're not, you're sunk. I think today's Yankees are real good examples of teamwork, because if you look at Joe Torre and his coaches, they value the team idea, and the players buy into it, too. They value on-base percentage over home runs. They hit behind the runner. They work deep pitch counts. They play team baseball. When Joe says, "We're a great team team," you know what he means.

You can learn a lot from teamwork in sports—mainly, you learn that anything can be achieved. The 1980 U.S. Olympic hockey team, they really worked together like a team. So did those two gals on the bobsled team in Salt Lake City. Nobody gave them a chance, but nobody knew how hard they worked together. When I was a coach on the 1969 Mets, everybody kept waiting for us to collapse. But we had somebody new each day doing something unusual. We had guys discarded by other teams, but they each contributed to the overall effect. If someone made an error, there was always someone to pick up his spirit. Teamwork was the big key.

If you're not a good team player, then you've got a problem. In the Navy during the war, I kept my mouth shut and obeyed orders. I was part of a six-man crew on a thirty-six-foot rocket boat for the Normandy landing, and everybody had to do their job or else. Mine was to fire a machine gun and help load the rocket guns. Our boat actually capsized some three hundred yards off-shore, but we all helped each other and we all luckily survived.

It's true that crisis brings out real teamwork, and that was true after 9/11. There was a real spirit around the country, with everybody pitching in, donating, helping any way they could. There was a big rise in volunteering. I think it made people think about helping and working together more— becoming more understanding of others. If it did, that's a pretty good thing.

"The Future Ain't What It **Used** to Be."

Things change. It's just the way it is. Bad things happen, times are different, but good things happen, too.

It's not good to always have your emotions go up and down—especially the bad emotions. It can eat you up. I bet most everybody gets angry day-to-day over something; they don't choose to be upset, but they do because they get mad. And it's OK to get mad. But whenever I get upset over something—like getting stuck in traffic, being lied to, hitting a bad golf shot—I ask myself, Is this worth having an ulcer about?

I try not to get too upset over things I can't control. People always do dumb things, and I've done my share. But it's like they say about spilling a glass of milk, there's nothing you can do about it. Just like when they were little kids, people get upset when they can't get what they want. I figure, you can do two things: Try harder to get it, or talk yourself out of wanting it so bad. That kind of worked for me.

Sometimes it pays to get upset—I think Casey Stengel used that philosophy just to push your buttons. Once he started giving me heck for how I called the pitches in a game we lost. I didn't mind it, but he kept it up and got pretty personal, and I finally blew my stack. "So if I'm doing so bad," I told him, "why don't you catch?" He didn't say anything to that and just walked into his office. But after we won the next day, and I went 3-for-4, he came over to my locker and gave me one of those sly grins, and said, "Got you mad, didn't I?"

When I played ball, the salaries weren't too good. Getting what I felt I deserved from the Yankees was a pretty big fuss, that's for sure. After my fourth season, I told George Weiss, our general manager, I didn't think it was fair to keep telling me that I was young yet and had a long time to make money. I also reminded him about the ninety dollars a month I'd made in the minors in Norfolk, and how the Yankees always told me if I did the job, I would get the money.

Well, I was doing the job. And I got a little upset after the 1950 season, when I hit .322 and we won our second straight World Series. Weiss thought my demand for $40,000 was crazy (I was making $18,000, the Yankees offered me $25,000) and he blasted me to the papers. He thought it was highway robbery. But then he called me up and said he'd compromise and we finally settled on $30,000. My holdout was over.

When I reported after spring training opened, one of the writers asked me if Weiss got mad. I said sure, but I think Casey finally talked him into giving me the money. Truth is, I only had a few contract squabbles. No question I'd get a little upset whenever the Yankees were trying to lowball me—they even made me take a cut after I had one so-so season (for me) after ten good ones. But I didn't get overly upset, just a little, and then I made sure I'd do better so I wouldn't have to get upset over the same thing again.

Just like life, baseball has joy and heartbreak, ups and downs, and always things to get upset about. There does seem to be a bit more anger in the game—on the field and off—than when we played. You can't pitch inside anymore, or the batter gets upset. I don't understand that. Even the fans, who are the ones who keep the game going, wind up feeling shafted because of how the owners and players keep bickering, threatening to shut down the game despite all their wealth. As a fan, I'd get kind of upset, too.

When I think about all the guys I played with, coached, or managed, everyone had different temperaments. Some hardly ever got upset, some couldn't control their emotions. Funny, look at the two Mickeys we had—Mickey Mantle and Mickey Rivers, both centerfielders but both with real different similarities. Mantle was a perfectionist who put great pressure on himself. He hit the longest home runs I've ever seen, but, boy, he could explode if he messed up. But Casey Stengel had a good way of getting Mickey to handle his rage. He'd give him a bat and tell him if he wanted to end his career, he should hit himself over the head and get it over with. I think that kind of humor is a good way to ease tension and anger; it helps put it in context.

When I joined the Yankees as a coach in 1976, we had some characters and Mickey Rivers was one of them. We called him "Gozzlehead"; I don't know why except that was his nickname. He was a hell of a lead-off hitter, that I know. He was also sort of in his own world, but that was good, because there was a lot of craziness around the team in those days. I remember he once had this quote: "I don't get upset over things I can't control, because if I can't control them, there's no use getting upset. And I don't get upset over the things I can control because if I can control them, there's no use in getting upset."

I know what he meant. There was a lot of turmoil in those days, fights and firings, and I simply tried to stay calm about the things I didn't like seeing. Everybody's sensitive whether they know it or not; lots of guys say they never get upset over what people say or write, but I'm not sure. When I later managed the Yankees, I wouldn't stay upset or mad too long. If I didn't like the way a guy was pitching, I'd tell him, but then I'd later check and see if he was mad at me for being mad at him. No question George Steinbrenner got me upset at times when he'd interfere and second-guess, and sometimes I didn't handle it that great. I felt that stress and began to smoke more. Looking back, getting fired wasn't the worst thing that happened. Whatever you do, working a high-pressure job for a difficult boss is a challenge. You're going to get upset, but how you handle getting upset will speak volumes about your ability to stay above it and succeed.

Thing is, it's always taken a lot to get me upset. It's all about perspective and what's important. If you find yourself getting upset a lot, you should do something about it— do things that make you feel good. Exercise. Play golf. Donate blood. Get more rest. Take a vacation. What you shouldn't do is ignore the problem. Don't feel sorry for yourself; don't smoke, eat, or drink too much; don't explode on other people. If you're in an argument, try to see the other point of view. If you don't agree, you don't agree; just don't let emotions get the best of you.

Maybe the maddest I ever got was arguing with the umpire when Jackie Robinson stole home in the 1955 World Series. They still show that tape over and over, with me really losing it with the umpire, Bill Summer. I was pretty darn hot, but I got over it pretty quick. It's easy to laugh about it today whenever it's brought up, because I know he was out—I didn't go crazy over nothing.

"It's Déjà **Vu** All Over Again."

Some situations are like recurring nightmares you have over and over. When I was managing the Yankees, we went through a bit of a losing stretch, and the writers kept asking me why we weren't winning, and finally I told them, "I wish I had an answer to that, because I'm tired of answering that question."

When things aren't going your way, when you're having tough times, and nothing you do seems to make much difference, that's when who you are down deep really comes out. At those times, all you have to fall back on are your most basic, truest beliefs—what you might call your values.

Your values are your own. Not everybody is going to be Mother Teresa, but the things you believe in should guide your actions and behavior. Maybe it's me, but I don't think you really get taught values—you learn them from living.

Whatever values I have come from what I experienced

on The Hill, where I grew up. I would've been just as juvenile as any juvenile delinquent today if it weren't for my family, St. Ambrose Church, and sports. St. Ambrose—that's where everybody went to Mass every Sunday morning unless you were flat on your back—influenced everything in our neighborhood. It's where all the spiritual and social activities happened: weddings, confirmations, funerals, war bond drives, you name it. More than anything, it promoted great pride among all the Italian families; everybody was real close-knit. When you were at St. Ambrose, you felt the importance of helping each other, working hard, and doing the right thing; when you were there you'd forget there was a Depression going on.

As a kid, I used to wonder why Pop worked so hard all the time. Now I know it was his Old Country values: discipline, responsibility, self-sacrifice, an honest day's work for an honest day's pay. He was setting an example for all of us. I learned that if you told Pop something, you'd better do it, and if he told you something, you'd sure as hell better obey. To this day I get pretty ticked if someone doesn't live up to his word. You say you're going to be there at five o'clock, you better be there at five o'clock no matter what time it is.

Sports was a tremendous thing for us, too. We were part of a gang—not those vicious gangs, just a bunch of us from the neighborhood playing whatever game was in season. We'd make our own rules and we'd play against other neighborhoods; that really helped us understand the importance of fair play, teamwork, and dedication. St. Louis was a soccer hotbed in those days, and we did our best to prove ourselves against the German, Irish, Spanish neighborhoods. As kids, sports energized us; it was a great outlet, and your success or failure was pretty much up to yourself. I always tell kids they can do anything they want as long as they're willing to work for it—the right way.

Everybody in business and sports, they all want success. Honesty is an important value, but sometimes you wonder. You wonder about people who take shortcuts, like kids who cheat in school. There's a good chance they become grown-ups who cheat in business, then get in trouble. Look at sports: There's such intense competition to succeed that guys feel they have to bulk up with these supplement things, which make some of them look like the Michelin Tire guy. Even if it's legal, I'm not sure it's right. Still, I think sports instill positive values in people: loyalty, pride, discipline, self-esteem.

Sometimes I'm not sure watching TV or video games is so good, because respect isn't a value you see a lot right now. I'm not big on people preaching their values—I think privacy is an important value, too—and I'm wary of phonies, people who say things they don't back up. But there are certain values I believe in for everybody, and I don't mind saying the Golden Rule is one—you know, Do unto others . . .

When you think about it, business is a lot like sports because you need to overcome things like defeats, tough competition, being undermanned, nobody giving you a chance. You have to care about a shared purpose, and each other. Good sports teams, like the Yankees, do that. I think values separate them from the others. They become resilient to setbacks and tough breaks because they don't go looking for someone else to blame. Instead they show character. I think of Mickey Mantle practically playing on one leg, because we needed him. And I think a few years ago of the Yankees losing Joe Torre for a while to cancer, then some of the players losing their fathers. They had the same qualities as a family, caring and pulling for each other. They were a good team, but they also had good values. That's what makes them successful, whether they win the last game of the World Series or not.

"The Other Teams Could Make Trouble
for Us If They **Win**."

It's no big secret—winning makes you feel better about everything, and losing doesn't. Everybody wants to win, who doesn't? Winning is important, that's why you keep score, but I think maybe overall it's gotten too much so, especially in kids' sports where there's too much stress on winning and not enough fun. I guess that's what's happened as sports have gotten so big in our country. Instead of asking their kids after a soccer or a Little League game, "Did you win?" maybe the parents should ask, "Did you give it your best?" or "Did you have fun?"

Too many kids are getting the message that if you're not a winner, you're a loser. That's not right. Kids' sports are different than professional sports—the pros are about winning and making money. I always thought kids playing sports, organized or pickup, should be about having fun, making friends, working on skills, becoming a better person. When kids start feeling pressure to win, they'll eventually drop out. I wish some adults would realize that. I've seen some of them at my grandkids' games—they're too overbearing, yelling all the time, telling them to do this, do that. Parents should just teach kids the fundamentals, and then encourage them to enjoy and love the game. And anyway, a game isn't the time to try to teach a kid how to do something; you save that for when you're practicing.

It's fun to compete, and it's even more fun to win. That I won't deny. But like I said, sports have gotten so big, with so much at stake, that people's values are affected. There seems to be a lot of cheating, misconduct, and bad fan behavior, because of the pressures and big money. Even in the Olympics, where they preach fairness and honor in competing against the world's best, things get kind of unethical. But I really think sports can teach a lot; it can teach you a lot about yourself. It can help you learn to win at important things. If you're going to win or succeed at anything, you're going to need discipline, confidence, steady, honest effort, and usually teamwork.

I learned that in my days with the Yankees, and even in business. During my baseball career, I got involved as a vice president at Yoo-Hoo, the chocolate drink company, and Phil Rizzuto and I were partners in a bowling alley in the 1950s and 1960s. All the things that helped us win with the Yankees were important there, too. No one person dominated everyone; you needed great effort and people sharing a common purpose. Like any team, you made the most of what you had, not what you lacked. As a catcher and then as a manager, you're kind of a boss, which is kind of like management, so you learn to treat everyone a bit different, to bring out their best. Some you get angry at, some you pat on the back. Know who you're dealing with and what's best for them.

I appreciated winning, and I was real fortunate to win a lot with the Yankees. I was in fourteen World Series in seventeen years, that's not too bad. Winning became a habit, because we had a winning attitude that came from the older guys, like Joe DiMaggio and Tommy Henrich. And we taught it to the younger guys—kind of like the Yankee Way—and the winning got contagious. The Red Sox had some real good teams, but I think maybe we had more unity and motivation in those days. Those World Series checks were like our extra salary, and we kinda counted on making that extra money, which was a little extra incentive. Funny thing is, the year we won the most games was 1954 when we won 103, but we still came in second to Cleveland. No excuses; you can't win all the time, and sometimes there's someone out there better than you. Like I said, the great thing about Casey was that when we were going good, he'd badger you pretty good; he'd always keep you sharp, never let you get complacent. And if we were going bad, he'd find ways to lift you up.

Winning taught me a lot. Mostly it taught me to be gracious and appreciative of being on the right team in the right place at the right time. I was never one to gloat, because that's just dumb. No matter how much we won I never thought, "I'm better than you are." Also, I never thought you had to be on a winning team to be a winner. I used to 'kid Ted Williams about never having to worry about having his World Series rings stolen, but the truth is, nobody respected his preparation and effort and skill more than me. He worked his heart out to be the best, and that's all you could ask for in anybody.

To me, winning is mostly in your mind. I used to say 90 percent of this game is half-mental, meaning that winning is really a want, a desire, and an attitude. Anyone trying to win or achieve something, on the playing field or in business, had better feel it's worthwhile—worthwhile enough to really commit yourself. Baseball's crazy with statistics, but there's no statistic for measuring mental attitude. How can you measure confidence? If you're a batter, how do you count not worrying about what pitcher you're facing? I'll just say that winning isn't always winning. Not everyone can be the winner. Some things don't always work out the way you plan. The main thing is to keep trying, do better next time, and deal with disappointment if it comes.

"He's Learning Me His **eXperience.**"

I was a so-called Depression baby. Then I became part of the so-called World War II generation. My sons became so-called baby boomers. And their kids—my grandchildren—are so-called Generation X, but I'd never call them that. They're kids, not letters.

It's too easy to put a label on a group, then assume you know everything about them. When I kept hearing about Gen X this and Gen X that, I asked Carm what a Gen X person is supposed to look like. She said they're kids who wear baggy pants and baseball caps backward, and I said that's great, I spent my career looking like that.

She said they're kids supposedly born around 1963 to 1981 who are confused all the time. I just can't believe so many kids are so mixed up. Anyway, they supposedly hang out in coffee places when they're not working at the Gap.

Supposedly they don't care about anything. Well, I don't know about that. Maybe they've just gotten a bad rap.

They're different these kids, that's true. My grandkids all use computers and other gizmos—that's the big thing these days. They're smarter because they have so much information—they're all information-happy, most of them. They don't grow up on baseball anymore, or most don't. There's a lot of different sports and they have a lot more outlets. Skateboarding, dirt-jumping on bikes, daredevil stuff, and other things you never heard of. But when we were kids we played games you never hear of anymore, either, like Indian Rubber or Johnny-on-the-Pony.

Funny how everybody gets tagged or stereotyped. Kids today are supposed to have a live-for-today way of thinking. They're supposed to want everything handed to them, but that's another wrong perception that isn't true. As kids we got stereotyped bad, too. When we played in the YMCA league on The Hill, we didn't have uniforms; the other teams, the ones with uniforms, would say, "Watch out for the dago kids, they'll steal your gloves." We also supposedly were aimless, like we didn't know what the heck we wanted to do with our lives. That was wrong, especially in my case—I may have been young and immature, but I knew all along I wanted to be a major-league player. And when I got there, I paid attention to people who knew more than I did, like Bill Dickey, who taught me how to be a real big-league catcher.

I think kids nowadays are smarter than they get credit for. They're more independent and individualistic. They have more real-life knowledge and can handle more difficult stuff that comes along. A lot of them are willing to work real hard, even though you always hear they're all slackers.

Just look at sports: Tiger Woods, Michael Jordan, and Derek Jeter all came from that generation and they didn't come out too shabby. If anyone was a slacker, it might've been me: I left school in eighth grade, though it wasn't un-usual for a teenager in the 1930s to get a job to help bring in money for the family. Problem was I couldn't keep a job—I kept getting fired because I was always cutting out early to find a baseball game to play in.

Today's generation of kids aren't that different from kids of other times, I think. I just think people always get both-ered by the styles of the latest generation. It doesn't bother me. But I really don't understand why a lot of them wear flannel shirts in summer—or their pants hanging down with their underwear showing. Whenever I see that, boy, I just think what my father would've done to me if I looked like that. But if that's the way they want to look, that's up to them.

The world is different, so things don't stay the same too much. People always ask me and other guys about today's players, and they are a bit different. For one, they don't have to work in the off-season, like a lot of us did. But they have great talent and dedication; they work at what they do all the time. Sure they get more money, but I think they respect the game and appreciate how lucky they are. Unfortunately, some don't know the history, some don't know the important things they should know. The Yankees had a catcher in spring training last year, and he asked for a lower uniform number than the one he'd been given. When the clubhouse guy asked what he had in mind, the player said, "How about Number 5?" He was then asked if he'd ever heard of a guy named DiMaggio.

Overall I guess this X Generation, or Generation X or whatever they call it, has one big thing in common with every other generation: It's coming of age in a changed world. Just don't undersell them and don't stereotype them. A lot of them can do some pretty good things. Besides, they still have something a lot of other generations don't have—and that's time.

"I Looked Like This When I Was **Young,** and I Still Do."

There used to be this saying, "It's great to be young and a Yankee." I don't know who said it first, but if I didn't say it when I was playing I should have.

Being part of the New York Yankees is something that's hard to describe. It feels like you're part of history. It's being connected to legends—Ruth, Gehrig, DiMaggio—and being part of a special family. Walking into Yankee Stadium for the first time, I felt like I was walking into something from the Bible. You always hear about the aura and mystique, but it's true: Playing there is like playing nowhere else. It's got the greatest prestige and exposure, and intensity and pressure like no other place. The fans won't let you forget who you represent, and neither will the owner. Dominance and dynasties—nobody comes close to the Yankees.

OK, I realize not everybody feels so mushy about the Yankees. People really hate them, I know that. But that's also what makes them so unique: they stir strong feelings both ways. People think they're lordly. They don't like it that they always have the resources to get the player they want. But the Yankees have always had smart baseball men and scouts, and usually invest their money smartly. Expectations are the highest with the Yankees. There's more media here, and more pressure to win. There's a tradition of it and that's the way it'll always be. To those who are jealous of all the success and all the championships, I'll just say two words: too bad.

I think businesses look at the Yankees as a model. Who wouldn't want to be dominant in their field? Who wouldn't want pride in their organization? Who wouldn't want to be the best? With the Yankees, it goes back to Babe Ruth; he brought people to the game that never saw a game before. He was larger than baseball; he was a phenomenon. He started the Yankee dynasty and made them the Number 1 box office attraction. I only met him once, my rookie year in 1947, but how can I forget it? It was before a game in St. Louis, about a year before he died. He was weakened and had a croaking voice, but I was awestruck; he was still an incredible presence. I shook his hand and I was pretty nervous. Imagine a kid putting on the same uniform worn by Ruth and Lou Gehrig—believe me, wearing the pinstripes does something to you.

So many great players have passed through that clubhouse. When you think about Gehrig, you think about a real American hero and that farewell speech about being "the luckiest man." His appreciation day became the first Old-Timer's Day—and the Yankees are the only team still keeping that going. DiMaggio became the symbol of the Yankees after Gehrig, and he symbolized grace and class. Joe took the greatest pride in being a Yankee, and that gets handed down year after year, generation after generation. When the players today go into the clubhouse, they pass a sign with DiMag's quote: "I want to thank the Good Lord for making me a Yankee."

Everyone can't help but know what he means. I remember when Casey took over in 1949, he used to tell us younger guys, "Don't ever forget, once you put on that shirt with the Yankee emblem on it, you become a Yankee and you stay a Yankee. Great things are expected of you just because you're wearing that uniform. Don't ever let it down. If you do you won't be a Yankee for long." We must've listened pretty good because we won five straight championships.

I got some ridicule from the writers and other players when I first joined the Yankees because I didn't look like a Yankee. I guess that meant that Yankees weren't short or looked like me. But that didn't bother me—I knew I didn't hit with my face. I just concentrated on being a good ballplayer and helping us win. I was lucky to be at the right place at the right time, so I got to play with great players during great years when we won a lot. Somewhere along the line I said, I'd rather be the Yankees' catcher than the

President, and I meant it. Being a Yankee and being in New York, you were treated great. The best part was the camaraderie; we truly felt like a family, always pulling for each other. We did everything together, played cards, went out and had our fun, but we always took baseball seriously. Those World Series shares were real important to us and we looked forward to that extra check every fall.

No other team has a history of helping each other like the Yankees. Every spring there are guys from past Yankee teams helping the current guys. I mentioned Bill Dickey coming out of retirement to work with me in spring training in 1949; I always say I'd never be the catcher I became if not for Dickey. Tommy Henrich did a great job in 1951 helping make Mickey Mantle a pretty good outfielder—remember, Mickey was nineteen and a shortstop and had never played the outfield until DiMaggio announced in spring training it was his last year. Go to spring training today and you'll see guys like Guidry and Mattingly and Reggie all doing the same thing: passing on their experience.

The players may change, but the uniform and the mystique don't. When the Yankees were recruiting Jason Giambi, they asked me to call him to tell him how much he'd love being a Yankee. I didn't mind because he's a good kid, and I thought he'd be pretty darn good playing in Yankee Stadium. I told him he'd be playing for a great manager with great teammates, he'd love the short porch in right, and he'd be playing in front of great fans. It wasn't a hard sell because his father is one of those Yankee fans who grew up idolizing Mickey Mantle. At Jason's press conference at the Stadium, he got kind of emotional and said, "We made it, Pop." A kid from California who always dreamed of being a Yankee. And who could blame him?

"You Saw Dr. **Zhivago?** Why? Aren't You Feeling Well?"

Whatever you do, you should do it with feeling. What I mean is, don't go through the motions. Whatever job you have, do it with real energy and effort, or else you won't get it done or done right. Doesn't matter if you're a ditch-digger or toll-taker or receptionist, you got to show some life. The more zest you have, the better job you'll do, the better you'll feel about it, and the better you'll make others feel.

If you don't like what you do or embrace it as a challenge, how can you do any good at it? The most successful people are the ones who have a passion for what they do. They never get bored, they still look forward to their work, and that's what keeps them going. Sometimes you can see it in their faces. Look at a guy like Don Zimmer, who's getting up there in age but you'd never know it except for his body, which isn't getting any younger. Zim's been in baseball for over fifty years, but he still lives and breathes the game despite the travel and the grind of all those long seasons. I know Zim still takes real pride in getting into the uniform every day, and he's still as dedicated and enthusiastic preparing for ballgames as he was thirty years ago.

People like Zim are what make baseball great. They still have a zest for what they do. They love being at the ballpark, love the game, love talking about it. Zim also loves playing the horses and still does—it's hard to give up something you've loved so long. I guess no matter what field you're in, if you lose your passion, it's probably time to retire or find something else.

Some people have a zest for life, which usually means they're happier than most people. Some have a zest for food, which likely means they're heavier, unless they watch their weight. But at least they have that enthusiasm, and that can tell you a lot about a person's disposition. Thing is, life should be satisfying—you should have a joy and energy that gives you a passion and purpose. Life is kind of what it is. Yours can be whatever you make it.

People always said I *loved* baseball, because I did. I still do. To me, it was the greatest experience of my life, because you have a tremendous sense of participation. It was a thrill to compete. You get a real feeling of pride helping to achieve something. After my first couple of years, I learned how to play with injuries, because I never wanted to come out of the lineup. Sure my energy would get worn down—Casey having me catch doubleheaders was no picnic—but I still kept my enthusiasm for the game. Once you entered that locker room, you'd get that spirit of feeling like a young boy, and that's what kept you going.

I can't play anymore, but I've never lost that zest for baseball, watching it, reading about it, talking about it. Overall I still enjoy lots of things. I'm an early riser, enjoy my morning coffee and reading the newspapers, and hopefully play a round of golf. Golf as well as my weekly card games and spending time with my family are the things I never tire of, and that's the way it's been for a while. If that's boring, it's not boring to me.

We all know certain people who have a zest for something and they never lose it. I remember some of the old ticket people, ushers, and clubhouse guys at Yankee Stadium—they always had that spark, that pride in what they did. Baseball-wise, I always enjoyed watching guys who exemplify that, too. Guys like Dave Winfield, whom I managed on the Yankees and who played as hard as he could every single night, and Don Mattingly, who never lost his great desire even when he battled his bad back. Back in my day, I remember Dizzy Dean, whose zest for the game was contagious; the whole Gas House Gang played with that little extra.

When I was a young player, I loved to watch Satchel Paige, who was older than everybody and still a character, real loosey-goosey, a showman, yet real proud and serious. Today so many of the Latin American players are great to watch. Many grew up playing baseball with rolled-up tape and a wooden stick, so it's more than a sport to them—it's something bred into them, giving them a chance to be somebody someday. Someone like Sammy Sosa still carries that enthusiasm—it's genuine and makes everybody feel better.

You'd be surprised how someone can affect others on the job in the slightest ways. A couple of years ago on the Yankees, Joe Torre called in Bernie Williams, who's kind of quiet, and everybody knows doesn't make a lot of noise. But Joe didn't like the way he was playing centerfield because he wasn't showing enough life—or, as he said, not showing his old zest and zeal for the game. And Joe told him that bothered him, because guys on the Yankees looked up to Bernie as one of the leaders. When Bernie heard that, I think it struck home because he got his old zest back right away.

Even if you could play baseball well without that zest for the game, why would you want to? Whether you love what you do or you do what you love, you're better off enjoying your life while you can, because you'll be dead for a long time and it doesn't sound like much fun.